THERAPY
101

A Brief Look at Modern Psychotherapy Techniques & How They Can Help

JEFFREY C. WOOD, PSY.D.
MINNIE WOOD, NP

New Harbinger Publications, Inc.

Publisher's Note

Care has been taken to confirm the accuracy of the information presented and to describe generally accepted practices. However, the authors, editors, and publisher are not responsible for errors or omissions or for any consequences from application of the information in this book and make no warranty, express or implied, with respect to the contents of the publication.

The authors, editors, and publisher have exerted every effort to ensure that any drug selection and dosage set forth in this text are in accordance with current recommendations and practice at the time of publication. However, in view of ongoing research, changes in government regulations, and the constant flow of information relating to drug therapy and drug reactions, the reader is urged to check the package insert for each drug for any change in indications and dosage and for added warnings and precautions. This is particularly important when the recommended agent is a new or infrequently employed drug.

Some drugs and medical devices presented in this publication may have Food and Drug Administration (FDA) clearance for limited use in restricted research settings. It is the responsibility of the health care provider to ascertain the FDA status of each drug or device planned for use in their clinical practice.

Distributed in Canada by Raincoast Books

Copyright © 2008 by Jeffrey C. Wood, Psy.D. and Minnie Wood, RN, NP

    New Harbinger Publications, Inc.
    5674 Shattuck Avenue
    Oakland, CA 94609
    www.newharbinger.com

Cover design by Amy Shoup; Text design by Amy Shoup and Michele Waters-Kermes; Acquired by Tesilya Hanauer; Edited by Kayla Sussel

---

Library of Congress Cataloging-in-Publication Data

Wood, Jeffrey C.
  Therapy 101 : a brief look at modern psychotherapy techniques and how they can help / Jeffrey C. Wood and Minnie Wood.
    p. cm.
  Includes bibliographical references.
  ISBN-13: 978-1-57224-568-6 (pbk. : alk. paper)
  ISBN-10: 1-57224-568-9 (pbk. : alk. paper)
  1. Psychotherapy--Popular works. I. Wood, Minnie. II. Title. III. Title: Therapy one hundred one. IV. Title: Therapy one hundred and one.
  RC480.515.W66 2007
  616.89'14--dc22

                    2007051522

10   09   08

10   9   8   7   6   5   4   3   2   1   First printing

To my parents, for their unending love, support, and encouragement.
—Minnie

To my wife, Minnie Wood, RN, NP, for all of her unending love,
support, and encouragement.
—Jeff

Contents

Foreword

There are many brands of psychotherapy, just as there are many brands of cars and appliances. Therapists call their brands theoretical orientations. And just like autos and toasters, some work better than others. Some are appropriate for certain conditions and not others.

What is a consumer to do? There is a bewildering array of psychotherapy brands (orientations) and virtually no consumer information on what works best for which problem. You end up having to choose a therapist without the slightest idea of whether this person can help you—or whether his or her brand of therapy helps anybody.

That's why psychotherapy consumers need this book. Many brands of psychotherapy work only for specific problems. If you have a different kind of problem, you'll get zero help. Take panic disorder (PD), for example. Psychodynamic therapy doesn't work for it. You could spend five years talking about your mother or father, but your panics won't get any better. The reason for this is that PD is reinforced and maintained by avoidance patterns. And the only kind of therapy equipped to help you overcome the avoidance patterns imbedded in PD is cognitive behavioral therapy.

Let's take a look at how the same two brands of therapy would be with a different problem. Suppose you're struggling with a lot of interpersonal difficulties. Your relationships are unsatisfying and frequently get into trouble, with the same behaviors and patterns emerging again and again. Although cognitive behavioral therapy might have relatively little to offer you, psychodynamic therapy may give you the means to examine the roots of your problem and the awareness necessary to change how you interact with others.

A lot of therapists don't want to admit that their brand of therapy is limited, that it won't work for everyone. So they gladly sign up any client who comes to them, hoping to help but not having a brand of therapy that's really equipped to do the job. Consumers struggling with psychological problems get damaged by the ignorance or false optimism of many practitioners.

There's something else you should know about psychotherapy brands. Some of them don't work for any problem. They're completely fraudulent. At best, they may help you understand more about your feelings or your inner life. But if you're struggling with anxiety, depression, eating disorders, ADD, trauma, anger problems, or any one of a host of other specific disorders, they have absolutely nothing to offer.

That's why you need this book. It is a consumer digest of psychotherapy brands. It describes how each treatment orientation works, what the therapy is like, and the basic treatment steps or components. Then, and this is what makes the book so valuable, it summarizes what the scientific research states about the therapy's effectiveness—not what its practitioners want to believe but what the *empirical evidence* says about its usefulness.

If you want to know about the full array of available therapies, this book is for you. If you want to know which therapy will work for your particular problem, this book will be an important resource. If you want to know which bogus therapies to avoid, again you have come to the right place.

Life is too short, and often our psychological pain is too great, to lose months or years working with brands of therapy that won't help you. This book will give you the knowledge you need to make the right choice for getting the help you need—now.

—Matthew McKay, Ph.D.
Author of *Thoughts & Feelings*

Introduction

WHY YOU NEED THIS BOOK

There are many reasons why we—Minnie and Jeff (your authors)—think that you should read this book. Nearly every day, we meet people who need help with their mental health problems, but they don't know where to start. Sometimes their problems are very serious, like depression, bipolar disorder, or schizophrenia, and other times they're normal, everyday issues that affect everyone (even us), like changes in jobs, relationship issues, stress, or worries about the future. Any of these people's stories would make a good introduction to this book.

But just as we started to write *Therapy 101*, Jeff had the following conversation with one of his clients, and we think it serves as a pretty good example of why this book is important. Here's what happened to Jeff:

"Recently, one of my new clients looked at me with a funny expression when I told him that there were well over one hundred different kinds of psychotherapies. 'What do you mean?' he asked.

"I explained that not every therapist was going to tell him to lie down on the couch and talk about his experience growing up, as we often see on television.

"He looked even more confused. Apparently, that was the only kind of treatment he was familiar with. 'So which one are we going to use?' he asked.

"'That depends on what's bothering you,' I responded."

Jeff explained to his client that there's no one cure-all therapy, no single psychological treatment that's effective for every problem. The type of treatment your therapist uses should be determined by the types of symptoms you're struggling with. At least, it should when you're working with a competent mental health professional. Unfortunately, there are some incompetent professionals out there who are more than willing to use the same treatment on every problem—and client—who walks into the office.

Imagine your primary care provider (PCP) doing the same thing, and whether you came in with a broken leg or a bad rash, your PCP giving you the same treatment. You'd never go back and you'd probably never get better. But most people know even less about psychotherapy than they do about medical treatments, which is why we wrote this book, to educate you, the consumer, about what you can expect when you go looking for therapy.

But let's get back to the client who walked into Jeff's office that day. "He told me that he was having some aches and pains in his shoulders and stomach and many anxious thoughts that preoccupied him most of the time. He worried about everything in his own life, many things in his friends' lives, and a few things in the lives of people he had never even met. It sounded like he was struggling with generalized anxiety disorder, a common form of anxiety that affects millions of people around the world but a problem that is also very treatable.

So, after he told me a little more about the problems he was having, I suggested that we use acceptance and commitment therapy (ACT), and maybe some biofeedback. I explained that ACT is a form of behavior therapy that uses mindfulness skills and explores a person's values and goals to help create a more fulfilling life. I also explained that biofeedback uses instruments to measure a person's physiological responses to stress so that he can learn to measure and control those responses and, hopefully, his stress too.

He said that he'd been in therapy for fifteen years before, and no one had ever talked to him about what he was going to do. I apologized for all those therapists who came before me.

'Why didn't they explain these things to me?' he asked.

Unfortunately, I didn't know."

We don't think therapists keep secrets from their patients to be mean, but we do think that some therapists, practicing some kinds of psychotherapy, don't explain the process of what's happening during the treatment because they don't want to "show their cards." That is, they think that if the patient knows what they, the therapists, are trying to accomplish, it will spoil the process. We disagree with this idea and so do many other psychotherapists.

Again, imagine walking into your PCP's office with a broken leg and she doesn't tell you what she's going to do. Instead, she just nods her head and listens to you talk about "how" you broke your leg and tells you nothing about what you can do to help it heal. Wouldn't that make you angry? And yet, despite the fact that there are dozens of very effective psychological treatments for most mental health problems, there are still some therapists who don't use these treatments. That's why you need this book!

> *The time has come to demystify therapy and to let you know what works for your problem so you can go out and get it.*

We all need to become educated consumers of psychological treatments. The time has come to demystify psychological therapy and to let you know what treatment works for your particular problem so you can go out and get it.

In just this little book, we've described approximately fifty of the most common forms of therapy, so you'll know what to expect when you walk through the door of a mental health professional's office. But even more importantly, we've also included a list at the end of each description of a particular therapy highlighting the problems it's effective for treating, based on the findings of research studies.

Before you begin reading about the different kinds of treatments, we thought it would also be useful to give you a quick overview of some common mental health problems. These are the problems for which people most often seek treatment. So let's take a look at some problems that might bring you into a therapist's office in the first place.

SOME COMMON AND TREATABLE MENTAL HEALTH PROBLEMS

Millions of adults and children—in the United States and worldwide—suffer with mental health issues like depression and anxiety. Sadly, however, many of them never get the help they need. Some of them might not have access to care and some just can't afford care. Others might be afraid of the perceived stigma attached to being in therapy or using psychiatric medications. But we would bet those others just don't know there are effective psychological treatments for their problems.

Whatever the reason, not getting into therapy when you need it can be very damaging to your life. In 2005, Philip Wang and colleagues jointly published a study of over nine thousand people, revealing that some of them had waited as long as twenty-three years before seeking help for their mental health problems. That's a lot of unnecessary suffering, especially since it's been estimated that almost half the population of the United States will struggle with a mental health problem at some point in their lives.

Why suffer with something that's causing you pain when many of the psychological treatments found in this book have been proven effective for most of these problems? Haven't you suffered long enough?

The problems are not arranged in any particular order, although anxiety and mood disorders are definitely the most common. While you're reading, be aware that these descriptions are very brief and by no means complete, so don't diagnose yourself with a mental health problem based solely on these descriptions. Only a trained mental health professional can help you do that. Rather, use these simple descriptions to help you recognize what your problem—or someone else's—*might* be, so you can use that information to point you in the direction of finding the right treatment. Also, be aware that it's possible, and even likely, that you are struggling with more than one of these problems at the same time, which makes it even more important for you to find the correct treatment.

Anxiety Disorders

Of all the mental health problems, *anxiety disorders* are the most common. In 2001, the National Institute of Mental Health estimated that they affect approximately 18 percent of the adult population every year and approximately 29 percent of all adults at any point in their lives.

Panic disorder is characterized by extremely powerful feelings of fear and anxiety that can quickly overwhelm you. These *panic attacks* include the physical symptoms of rapid heart rate, hyperventilating, and feeling faint, and they often last ten to fifteen minutes. They are also frequently accompanied by *agoraphobia*, or a fear of leaving home.

A *specific phobia* is an intense, overwhelming, irrational fear of something identifiable, such as an animal, insect, situation, or place. *Social phobia*, or *social anxiety disorder*, is an intense fear of being humiliated in front of other people.

Obsessive-compulsive disorder (OCD) is characterized by uncontrollable, disturbing thoughts and urges called *obsessions*, which make you feel extremely anxious. Then, in response, you might perform repetitious, time-consuming behaviors called *compulsions* to relieve the anxiety.

Post-traumatic stress disorder (PTSD) is a serious set of problems that occurs after you experience a potentially life-threatening event, such as rape, war, crime, a natural disaster, or an accident. Symptoms often include flashbacks, nightmares, heightened agitation, heightened awareness, thoughts about death, difficulty sleeping, and avoidance of people or related circumstances.

Generalized anxiety disorder (GAD) is characterized by an excessive number of unmanageable worries that don't go away, and it's often accompanied by difficulty sleeping, trouble concentrating, and muscle tension (especially in the head, neck, shoulders, jaw, or stomach).

Mood Disorders

Mood disorders are the second most common subset of mental health problems, affecting approximately 10 percent of the adult population every year and approximately 21 percent of all adults at any point in their lives. Currently, major depression is the most disabling mental health problem in the world. However, the World Health Organization estimates that by the year 2020, major depression will be the leading cause of disability among all mental *and* physical health problems both for women and for people living in developing countries.

Major depression is characterized by excessive feelings of sadness, a lack of pleasure in your life, trouble concentrating, difficulty sleeping (sleeping too much or too little), low levels of energy, unexpected changes in weight, and possibly thoughts about dying or suicide.

Bipolar disorder, formerly called *manic depression*, is characterized by excessively energetic or irritable moods called *manic episodes*. During a manic episode, you might feel excessively happy, restless, self-confident, impulsive, or distracted, and you might have trouble sleeping. You might also experience periods of depression in between manic episodes.

Drug and Alcohol Problems

Drug and alcohol problems account for another large portion of mental health problems, affecting approximately 4 percent of the adult population every year and approximately 15 percent of all adults at any point in their lives. Such related problems are usually defined in two different ways. *Substance abuse* is a troubling pattern of drug or alcohol use characterized by the use of the substance interfering with your work, school, home life, or relationships; drinking or using drugs in potentially dangerous situations (such as while driving); and continuing to drink or use despite related reoccurring legal problems.

Substance dependence, a more serious problem, also includes the development of *tolerance* to the effects of the drugs or alcohol, symptoms of *withdrawal* that occur if you stop drinking or using, an inability to cut down or control your use, as well as spending a large amount of time involved with your drinking or using drugs.

Relationship and Family Problems

It's impossible to know for sure how many people in the world are struggling with relationship and family problems, but a conservative estimate is that anyone who's ever had a family or a relationship has probably had a problem. (Does that leave anyone out?)

However, many serious relationship and family problems occur in marriages, domestic partnerships, couples, and families due to a variety of difficulties. These often include problems communicating effectively; expressing emotions; expressing needs; coping with the mental health problems of a spouse, partner, or family member; or as the result of long-standing patterns or habits established earlier in life.

> *A conservative estimate is that anyone who's ever had a family or a relationship has probably had a problem.*

Personality Disorders

A *personality disorder* is a long-standing style of behavior that interferes with your job, relationships, and social situations, or causes you great emotional distress. Approximately 15 percent of all adults struggle with a personality disorder.

Someone with *avoidant personality disorder* puts off making decisions because he or she is afraid of being criticized by others for making a "wrong" decision. People with *antisocial personality disorder* manipulate and abuse others for their own purposes, lie to get what they want, show little concern for the safety of others, and might even be violent or destructive.

Someone with *borderline personality disorder* experiences frequent and painful mood swings, great difficulty forming and maintaining relationships, problems controlling spontaneous and reckless behavior, and a fluctuating sense of self.

A person with *dependent personality disorder* is afraid of making decisions without the constant assistance and approval of other people. Those struggling with *histrionic personality disorder* often try to be the center of attention, exaggerate their emotions and the importance of relationships, and exhibit rapidly shifting emotions.

Someone who is described as having *narcissistic personality disorder* thinks that he or she has many more exceptional qualities than other people, expects to be treated in a special way because of a sense of entitlement, and often shows little empathy for others.

People with *obsessive-compulsive personality disorder* have rigid, internal demands for organization, control, and precision. Those suffering with *paranoid personality disorder* have a deep mistrust of other people and their motives, which makes it very difficult to form and maintain relationships.

A person who has *schizoid personality disorder* is not interested in developing social contacts or relationships and often prefers to be alone. People with *schizotypal personality disorder* are often seen as being eccentric or odd in the way they think, dress, speak, or behave, and they experience difficulty maintaining relationships despite wanting to have social connections.

Eating Disorders

Eating disorders will affect approximately 5 percent of all adults at some point in their lives, and most of these people will be women. *Anorexia* is characterized by an intense fear of gaining weight, excessively low body weight (approximately 85 percent or less of a normal, expected weight), and a restriction of your intake of calories. It might also involve binge eating; purging of food by vomiting, laxatives, or other means; and excessive exercise.

Bulimia is also characterized by an intense fear of gaining weight, periods of rapid and excessive binge eating, and purging of food by vomiting, laxatives, or other means. However, unlike anorexia, if you struggle with bulimia, you are probably close to a normal, expected weight.

Binge-eating disorder is similar to bulimia in that it involves uncontrollable periods of excessive and rapid binge eating, but it does not involve later purging of the food.

Schizophrenia

Schizophrenia is one of the planet's leading causes of disability. According to a 2001 report from the National Institute of Mental Health, it affects approximately 1 percent of the world's population. *Schizophrenia* is an illness caused by biological factors. It often causes hallucinations, delusions (mistaken beliefs), confused thinking and poor concentration, uninhibited or restricted behavior, jumbled speech, problems interacting with others, uncontrollable emotional reactions, and, possibly, a deep suspicion of others.

Impulse Control Disorders

A person with an *impulse control disorder* can't avoid doing something that might bring harm to him- or herself or to others.

Pathological gambling is repeated betting behavior that interferes with finances, job, family life, or other relationships. If you have *kleptomania*, you give in to urges to steal things that have no financial or personal value.

Pyromania is the repeated act of deliberately setting fires, for no financial gain, after which you feel relieved or excited. If you have *trichotillomania*, you experience a release of tension or satisfaction by pulling out your hair. If you have *intermittent explosive disorder*, you injure others or damage property when you suddenly and unexpectedly lash out in aggressive ways. Recently, Internet and computer-game addictions have also been thought of as impulse control disorders.

Somatoform Disorders

Somatoform disorders are a collection of mental health issues related to your perception of or the functioning of your body. These disorders affect a large number of people who often seek medical treatments, although all of these problems also involve some psychological issue.

Body dysmorphic disorder is characterized by an obsessive concern with a part of your body that you think is severely flawed or deformed. A *somatization disorder* is characterized by widespread chronic pain throughout your body, a sexual dysfunction, and/or stomach or digestion problems.

A *conversion disorder* is a problem with moving a part of your body or using one of your senses. A *pain disorder* involves severe pain in any part of your body that causes great disturbance in your life and is often accompanied by some type of depression or anxiety. And *hypochondriasis* is a sincere, persistent worry about being sick.

Anger Control Problem

It's difficult to know how many people are struggling with an anger control problem (but the way the world's going, it sure looks like a lot of people). An *anger control problem* can be identified when you frequently react in quick and aggressive ways after feeling insulted, wronged, or injured. You probably get easily infuriated when you think you're being mistreated, you "blow up" or "explode" at others, and afterward you might feel guilty about what you've done.

> *An anger control problem can be identified when you frequently react in quick and aggressive ways after feeling insulted, wronged, or insjured.*

Adjustment Disorder

It's also difficult to approximate how many people are struggling with adjustment disorders, but the estimates range from 10 to 30 percent of the people seeking treatment at mental health centers. An *adjustment disorder* is a sad or anxious reaction to a stressful situation that lasts longer than what is considered typical. It's different than *bereavement*, which is considered a normal reaction to the death of a loved one.

Problems First Seen in Childhood

Many problems that affect adults are first recognized in children as young as three to seven years old. These are just a few of them.

Attention-deficit/hyperactivity disorder (ADHD) affects approximately 3 to 7 percent of school-aged children and 1 to 5 percent of adults. ADHD is characterized by an inability to focus and sustain attention; an inability to control impulses, behaviors, and emotions; and a recurring feeling of restlessness.

Autism affects less than 1 percent of children and is characterized by impaired or absent social skills, great difficulties communicating, repetitive and limited interests and behaviors (such as rocking or spinning), and severely limited mental abilities. *Asperger's disorder* is similar to autism. A person struggling with Asperger's will also have great difficulty interacting in social situations, as well as repetitive and restricted interests and behaviors. However, he or she does not have trouble communicating and has, at least, a normal level of intelligence.

Conduct disorder has been observed in 1 to 10 percent of children, more often in boys, and is characterized by violent behavior toward other people or animals, lying, stealing, destroying property, and rule-breaking.

Dissociative Disorders

Dissociative disorders are a group of problems characterized by strange feelings of being detached from reality. *Dissociative amnesia* and *dissociative fugue* are two similar disorders marked by an inability to remember significant episodes of your life, with amnesia affecting a limited number of memories and fugue affecting your entire history.

Dissociative identity disorder, formerly called "multiple personality disorder," is the experience of having two or more distinct alternative personalities in your body that emerge at certain times. *Depersonalization disorder* is a problem characterized by a feeling of being disconnected from your body and/or your thoughts.

These disorders are the most common mental health problems that are often targeted by the psychological treatments found in this book.

THE CAST OF CHARACTERS ... UH, WE MEAN, PROFESSIONALS

Before you get started reading about the treatments, we also thought it would be helpful for you to know who you might meet when you begin psychotherapy, because not every therapist does the same job. In fact, the term "therapist" is generic, and it can be used by many different people performing fairly different jobs. A therapist is simply a person who performs some type of psychotherapy (like the ones found in this book), but therapists are also found in other professions, which makes the term a little confusing (physical therapist, massage therapist, speech therapist, and so on). For the sake of this book, we will be referring to one of the following types of mental health professionals whenever we refer to a psychotherapist or therapist.

Often, the first person you'll meet is your primary care provider, such as your medical doctor (MD) or nurse practitioner (NP), who normally treats you for general health problems. He or she is also trained to recognize and diagnose mental health problems and to prescribe medications for their treatment.

However, *psychiatrists* and *psychopharmacologists* are medical doctors who specialize in the treatment of mental health problems.

These professionals, as well as *psychiatric nurse practitioners,* are often more up to date about the best medications available for complex problems.

All of these medical professionals are most likely to treat your problem with medications, not psychotherapy, although, hopefully, they will also suggest therapy as an additional treatment for your problem. And if they don't, you should ask them about it.

For more information about psychiatrists, visit the website of the American Psychiatric Association at www.psych.org or www.healthy minds.org.

Psychologists (Ph.D., Psy.D., Ed.D.) are nonmedical doctors who are also experts in treating and diagnosing mental health problems. They are trained to assess mental health problems using psychological or neuropsychological testing. A psychologist will use one of the many forms of psychotherapy found in this book to treat a problem, but he or she cannot prescribe medications (with the exception of some specially trained psychologists in Louisiana and New Mexico). If you suspect that medications might be helpful to you, ask your psychologist, or other therapist, for a referral. (Also, see chapter 8, A Final Word About Medications.)

For more information about psychologists, visit the website of the American Psychological Association at www.apa.org or the *Psychology Today* website at www.psychologytoday.com.

A *master's level counselor* (MFT, MA) has earned a master's degree in psychotherapy and often focuses on treating couples and families, although many counselors also treat individuals.

For more information about master's level counselors, visit the website of the American Association for Marriage and Family Therapy at www.aamft.org.

A *social worker* (MSW, LCSW) has also earned a master's or doctoral degree and is an expert in case management and issues that might affect your mental health, such as poverty, physical abuse, substance abuse, unemployment, and disability. In addition, social workers often can provide individual and family therapy.

For more information about social workers, visit the website of the National Association of Social Workers at www.naswdc.org.

These are the most likely professionals you'll come across in your search for psychological treatments. However, some people seek help elsewhere, too, like from their priest, rabbi, imam, or minister. *Life coaches* are popular these days, too, as are *hypnotherapists*. And you always have the old standbys of friends, families, and strangers.

Whomever you choose to help you, make sure that person is qualified to treat your problem, unbiased in the help he or she offers, and has experience in treating the problem you're struggling with. If the person doesn't meet these qualifications, ask him or her for a referral to someone who does.

Plus, be aware that there are unqualified, unprofessional, and sometimes unscrupulous people out there who will claim that they are able to treat your mental health problem and will be more than willing to take your money. Be cautious of these snake-oil salespersons and don't expect quick answers to your long-standing problems. Stay away from those who claim that they can help you only if you give them more money. Beware of fake "experts" who claim that your current problems stem from your past lives or that the answers to your problems lie hidden in the cards that only they can read. Participate in these things if you want a good laugh, but not if you want help with your anxiety, depression, or any other mental health issue. Leave that work to the mental health professionals.

> *Beware of fake "experts" who claim that your current problems stem from your past lives or that the answers to your problems lie hidden in the cards that only they can read.*

HOW TO CHOOSE THE RIGHT THERAPIST FOR YOUR PROBLEM

We wish we could say that choosing the right therapist for your problem was going to be simple, but the truth is, it's going to take some effort on your part. After reading the descriptions of the therapies, hopefully, you'll have a better idea about the type of treatment you're looking for, which is the treatment that works best for your problems. Then, if you don't already have a recommendation for a therapist who offers that type of treatment, you can get a referral by:

■ Asking your primary care provider

■ Asking someone you know and trust who's been in therapy before

■ Contacting your insurance company

■ Contacting the national, state, or county association that governs the type of professional you're looking for, such as the American Psychological Association or the California Association of Marriage and Family Therapists.

■ Contacting an association of professionals that provides the type of treatment you're looking for, such as the Association for Behavioral and Cognitive Therapies or the EMDR International Association. (These websites are listed after the description of each therapy.)

When you eventually speak with a therapist for the first time, you should briefly explain the nature of your problem and why you're calling. Then ask a few basic questions such as, "Do you have experience treating problems like mine?" If the answer is no, ask the person for a referral to someone who does.

Also, be sure to ask about the type of treatment he or she might use for your problem. If the therapist suggests something you're not familiar with, ask the person to give you an idea of what it might involve. If the treatment doesn't sound like something you'd want to try, ask for a referral to someone else. Moreover, if the answer is vague and unfocused, ask for the specific steps of the treatment. If the therapist can't describe it very well, he or she may not know it very well. Again, ask for a referral to someone else.

And, finally, ask how much the treatment costs and whether they accept your insurance, if applicable. Most professionals charge per session, and prices vary as much by specialty as they do by state. Then, if you're satisfied with the answers you get, ask to make an appointment.

Don't expect to spend too much time on the phone talking with the person. You simply want to find out if the therapist has the skills and experience you're looking for to treat your problem.

HOW TO DETERMINE IF YOUR THERAPY IS WORKING

Now, let's assume that with the help of *Therapy 101* and a little time and energy spent on your part, you find the right therapy and the right person to work with … or so you think. How do you know if your therapy is helping you? The simple way is to ask yourself: "Do I feel better now compared to how I felt before I started?" If the answer is yes, that's a good indication it's working. But if the answer is no, then maybe it's time to think about trying something new.

But let's be more specific. Every few weeks you should reevaluate your therapy to determine if it's effective. If your therapist doesn't suggest this, you should. Make a plan with him or her to reevaluate what's happening after the first eight weeks of treatment. Collaboratively, decide on a reasonable goal to achieve by that time. Then, if you're not satisfied with your progress in eight weeks, discuss your concerns. Maybe your treatment goals need to be readjusted, or perhaps the form of therapy you've chosen isn't the right one for you and your needs.

However, be fair in your evaluation. You cannot expect complicated problems to disappear completely in only a matter of weeks. Consider how old you are, how long the problem has existed, and how deeply ingrained it is in your life. If your problem is long-standing, assume that the treatment will take significant time and effort to counteract your old patterns.

Also, be aware that you can judge the treatment accurately only if you've been attending your sessions regularly and doing what you and your therapist have agreed upon. If you haven't been doing those things, then you're just wasting your time and money. But if you've been following the treatment plan, you've been participating, and you're still not satisfied, ask your therapist for his or her opinion about what's happening. Again, either the treatment or your goals may need to be adjusted, or maybe you need to find a different form of treatment.

And remember (or take note): therapy doesn't mean forever. Just because you might need help now doesn't mean you'll have to be in therapy for the rest of your life. Good, effective therapy should help you learn how to better cope with the problem you came in with, but don't expect it to solve every problem in your life. That's impossible. Even good therapists and nurse practitioners (like your authors) have problems now and then.

> *Just because you might need help now doesn't mean that you'll have to be in therapy for the rest of your life.*

Look to your therapist as an expert teacher who's helping you cope more effectively with a part of life that you're struggling with. Don't make him or her into a guru who you're going to follow around for the rest of your life. Too often, we hear stories about clients who have spent over ten years with the same therapist, struggling with the same problems they had ten years ago. Most of these long-term clients stay in treatment because they've become dependent on the therapist instead of learning to cope with their problems on their own.

If you're working in a time-limited therapy like cognitive behavioral therapy or time-limited dynamic psychotherapy, most likely the treatment will come to a close after a predetermined goal has been reached. But if you're in an open-ended treatment, like psychoanalysis or existential therapy, here's a good basic rule to follow: if you don't notice improvements in six to twelve months in treatment, you should consider an alternate form of treatment or, at least, get a second opinion. But again, remember, different problems take different amounts of time to treat, and complex problems can take even longer. So you need to be your own best judge.

Set goals for yourself with your therapist and when you reach those goals, reevaluate whether you want to commit to further treatment. If your goal is to be able to make a public speech without having a panic attack, and you reach that goal, maybe you'll want to stop treatment. But if your problem is more widespread throughout your life, as it is in post-traumatic stress disorder following a trauma, maybe you'll want to work on several goals, such as stopping your nightmares, soothing your anxiety, reconnecting with people, going out again, and so forth.

Be compassionate with yourself as you begin the process of making changes in your life. It can sometimes be a slow process that takes work on your part, so be persistent. And when things get tough and you feel like giving up, remember your long-term goal of improving your life and why you're investing all this energy in the first place.

COMMON FACTORS OF DIFFERENT THERAPIES

Lastly, a word about the "therapy wars." You would think—or hope—that all mental health experts would share the same opinions about what works best in therapy. But that's far from the truth. There are many dissenting opinions arguing one way or the other about what treatment works best for your problem, but those arguments are way beyond the scope of this book.

However, as mental and physical health experts, we strongly suggest that you use this book to guide you in choosing the best therapy for your problem, and we refer you to the end of each therapy description to see whether that treatment will help you with the problem you're struggling with. As we said before, our suggestions are based on some of the most current research.

However, having said that, it's also interesting to note that researchers have found common factors among all successful therapies, no matter what school of thought they identify with. You can think of these factors as the essentials of what you're looking for in a successful treatment. Because no matter which therapy you choose to work in, you're going to be spending at least a few weeks or months (or longer) working with someone in an intimate setting. Naturally, you want that experience to be a positive and inspiring one.

Not surprisingly, a positive working relationship is one of the most important common factors of a successful therapeutic experience. "Shop" for a therapist the way you would shop for a used car: spend some time asking questions, go for a test drive, kick the tires (but not their shins!), and see if the relationship is a good match for your personality and purposes. Two of the factors that will probably determine a good fit will be your perception of how empathetic the therapist is with you and your situation and how competent he or she is at treating your problem.

But for your therapy to succeed, other factors need to be present too, and both you and your therapist have certain responsibilities to fulfill. In 1986, David Orlinsky and Kenneth Howard identified a number of other common factors that exist in successful therapies. First, you, the client, must be willing to discuss and explore your thoughts and feelings in treatment. Otherwise, your therapy sessions will just be two people sitting quietly in a room together. Second, there should be an agreement between you and your therapist about how the treatment will proceed. One of the most helpful things therapy does is that it provides you and your therapist with a framework for understanding your problem and determining what has to be done to improve it. Third, your therapist will use specific strategies to improve the problem that brought you into treatment, strategies that will vary from therapy to therapy. And lastly, a successful treatment will cause you, the client, to change in some way. This can be a subtle realization about how to do something differently in your life, or it might be a big "aha" moment that changes your life forever.

But, ultimately, what makes therapy effective and helps people change their minds and their lives? That's the big question, and each school of therapy will have a different answer. Cognitive behavioral therapy will help you confront your fears and challenge your negative thoughts. Acceptance and commitment therapy will help you redefine your life according to what you value. Psychodynamic therapy will help you gain insight into the origins of your problem. Solution-focused therapy will help you look for new answers to old problems. And so on. There's much debate about which common factor is the most responsible for change in a successful treatment. But, today, there's little debate that therapy itself can be successful.

In their seminal study of 1977, Mary Lee Smith and Gene Glass analyzed the results of 375 studies of multiple forms of psychotherapy and found that people who completed therapy were better off than 75 percent of the people who weren't receiving treatment. They had a reduction in fear and anxiety, increased self-esteem, improved social relationships, and better functioning at school and work.

Similarly, a 1995 study by *Consumer Reports* magazine conducted a survey of approximately four thousand people who sought treatment for a mental health problem. Eighty-seven percent who initially felt "very poor" and 92 percent of those who felt "fairly poor" said that they felt "somewhat" to "a lot" better after getting into therapy. These people felt more confident, had higher levels of self-esteem, and reported enjoying life more. The study also showed better treatment results for people who played an active role in their own therapies and for those who searched for a therapist who best fit their own needs.

So, now, you're already on your way to getting help. Reading *Therapy 101* is your first step in playing an active role in your own treatment and finding a therapist who will provide you with a good fit for your problems. In the rest of this book, you'll find brief descriptions of many different kinds of therapies. We suggest you read the entire book and find the treatment that sounds most appropriate for your problem. Near the end of the book, you'll also find some information about health and nutrition, as well as information about medications, which also might be important for your treatment, so make sure you read those chapters, too. Then, at the end of the book, we've included some humorous (and disturbing) information about a few treatments we think you should avoid.

Good luck with your journey into therapy. We both wish you success and a happier, more fulfilling life.

CHAPTER 1

Treatments Supported by Research

The effectiveness of the following treatments has been supported by studies comparing them to the use of other treatments and, often, the use of medications. All of these treatments will require you to collaborate with your therapist and to play an active role during your sessions. Some of these treatments are conducted in brief formats of eight to fifteen sessions, and many are conducted in a consistent, step-by-step manner.

Not all of the treatments in this book have been standardized or subjected to the same amount of research as the treatments discussed in this chapter. Not all treatments, like psychoanalysis, are capable of being standardized, so studying them is often difficult. Some competing clinicians would argue that conducting therapy in a consistent, standardized way is "cold" or "impersonal." However, this is more often the fault of the therapist than the therapy.

In this chapter you'll be introduced to behavior therapy, the treatment made famous by applying successes with laboratory animals to the lives of human beings. Brief psychodynamic therapy is a shorter, more standardized form of Freud's psychoanalysis. Cognitive behavioral therapy combines the successes of early behavior therapy with the newer insights of how thoughts affect actions. Interpersonal therapy examines the way your relationships affect the way you feel. And rational emotive behavior therapy, a treatment similar to cognitive therapy, will help you to untangle yourself from self-imposed rules and distorted ways of thinking.

BEHAVIOR THERAPY

Behavior therapy focuses on the way dysfunctional behaviors lead to mental health problems. One of the main beliefs of this treatment is that your actions and reactions are largely learned. Some behaviors are actively reinforced and rewarded with things like food and money, while other behaviors are learned by watching and imitating other people. Unlike a *cognitive behavioral* therapist, a therapist working from a strictly behavioral model is not interested in the way your thoughts affect your actions and emotions. However, today, a more flexible behavior therapist will often be indistinguishable from a cognitive behavioral therapist (which you can read about below).

Behavior therapy has gone through many changes. At the beginning of the twentieth century, early behavioral theory was largely influenced by the work of the famous Russian physiologist, and Nobel prize winner, Ivan Pavlov. Pavlov discovered that the dogs used in his research experiments salivated both when they saw their food and when they heard the ringing of a bell that announced the arrival of their food. In the dogs' brain, the association of the food and the bell had become the same, and therefore, they both elicited the same physical response.

Later, in the 1950s, the American psychologist B. F. Skinner brought behavioral theory to the forefront of psychology. Skinner used similar types of reinforcement such as food and punishment to shape the behavior of animals, and later humans. Both of these researchers

Bad little therapist. John B. Watson, the "father of American behaviorism," is infamously remembered for his 1920 "Little Albert" experiment, in which he conditioned an eleven-month-old boy to fear white rats, dogs, and Santa Claus masks. Shortly after, Watson became a very successful advertising executive at J. Walter Thompson.

> *The focus of behavior therapy is on the here and now and what can be done to help you solve your problems.*

greatly influenced the learning theories of what later became behavior therapy.

Behavior therapy focuses on actions that can be observed. Factors that cannot be observed, such as unconscious thoughts, are unimportant to this treatment. The focus of behavior therapy is on the here and now and what can be done to help you solve your problems. Behavior therapists aren't concerned with helping you figure out what may have caused your problems. In some ways, behavior therapy is like an urgent medical treatment. Your primary care provider isn't concerned with *how* you broke your leg; rather, he or she will focus on what can be done to fix it.

Like the other therapies in this chapter, behavior therapy is based on research that has determined the most effective procedures to treat a particular mental health problem. As a result, the treatment for each problem will be slightly different. For example, the treatment for depression will be different than the treatment for phobias. All of the treatments are structured and time-limited, but they are also very interactive. In session, you and the behavior therapist will work as collaborators, identifying the nature of your problem, what triggers it, and how long it lasts. Then the two of you will come up with a treatment plan, to which you'll be asked to commit.

The methods used in behavior therapy will depend on the nature of your problem, but often they include relaxation exercises, training in assertive communication skills, problem-solving skills, and role playing to learn new social skills. You'll also be asked to record your behaviors during the week outside of session, in order to observe your progress.

Again, depending on your problem, your therapist also might ask you to engage in activities that often seem challenging, such as using *exposure and response prevention*. This method, which is used to treat obsessive-compulsive disorder, requires you to make a list of your feared situations. Then, in a safe, systematic way, you'll be asked to expose yourself to the feared events, either in real life or in your imagination, beginning with the least fearful situation and working your way up to the most frightening. The goal of this treatment is to help you successfully confront your fears in a safe, progressive way and to help you realize that nothing bad or dangerous will happen to you.

Behavior therapy is effective for treating:

- Attention-deficit/ hyperactivity disorder (ADHD)
- Autism
- Childhood developmental disorders
- Depression
- Obsessive-compulsive disorder
- Schizophrenia-related issues
- Sleep disorders

For more information, visit the websites of:

- The Association for Behavioral and Cognitive Therapies: www.abct.org
- The National Association of Cognitive-Behavioral Therapists: www.nacbt.org

Now you try it: *If you have a pet, or a gullible friend, play Pavlov for a few days. Ring a bell before feeding your subject every meal for a week. Then observe how your subject will come running when most any bell is rung, even if it's not a regular mealtime.*

BRIEF PSYCHODYNAMIC THERAPY

Brief psychodynamic therapy is a form of treatment largely based on psychoanalysis. However, as the name of this therapy suggests, the length of the treatment is much shorter than traditional psychoanalysis. Typically, the number of sessions will range from five to forty. The session limit will be discussed before treatment begins, and it's likely that your psychotherapist will often remind you of the termination date.

The term "brief psychodynamic therapy" actually includes a number of different treatments, each with a slightly different focus. Some concentrate on making connections between your past childhood experiences and your current problems. Others closely examine your thoughts and feelings about your psychotherapist or discuss what it feels like to end treatment so soon. Most of these elements are also explored in traditional psychoanalysis. However, you can expect your brief psychodynamic therapist to be more interactive with you in session. He or she also will provide you with more feedback than you'd normally get in traditional psychoanalysis.

The goal of most of these brief psychodynamic therapies is to resolve one or two major problems in your life. For this reason, brief psychodynamic therapy might be a good treatment for you if you already have some insight about your problem and you're open to talking about it.

One of the brief psychodynamic therapies that has received some research support is *time-limited dynamic psychotherapy* (TLDP), developed by psychologist Hanna Levenson. TLDP also incorporates elements of interpersonal therapy and cognitive behavioral therapy, but unlike traditional psychoanalysis, TLDP sets clear goals for treatment.

Sometimes shorter is better. Many of Sigmund Freud's most famous, psychoanalytic cases were actually very brief. In the case of "Katharina," Freud needed only one informal session to cure the young woman of her anxiety, when he helped her uncover two repressed memories of her uncle's attempts to molest her.

One of the objectives of TLDP is to identify repetitive problems and long-standing bad habits that get in the way of creating healthy, fulfilling relationships. Your TLDP therapist will briefly help you explore your past relationships and traumas to determine the origin of these patterns and habits, but most of the time the treatment's focus will be on helping you resolve those issues by developing new ways of behaving in relationships.

The relationship between you and your therapist will even be used as an opportunity to help you practice your new skills. You should expect your TLDP therapist to draw your attention to how you act in session and to how you treat him or her. By engaging in this process, the ultimate goal of TLDP is to provide you with a new and improved relational experience so that you can begin thinking of yourself in a healthier way and begin engaging in more fulfilling relationships.

Brief psychodynamic therapy can be effective for treating:

- Anorexia
- Antisocial personality disorder
- Dependent personality disorder
- Depression
- Narcissistic personality disorder
- Post-traumatic stress disorder
- Schizoid personality disorder

For more information, visit the website of:

- Hanna Levenson, Ph.D.: www.hannalevenson.com

> **Now you try it:** *Record your five worst habits and describe how they interfere with your relationships. What needs to be changed and how could you do it?*

COGNITIVE BEHAVIORAL THERAPY

Cognitive behavioral therapy (CBT) is a form of treatment that combines elements of *behavior therapy* and *cognitive therapy*. Behavior therapy examines the way your actions affect your mental health, while cognitive therapy looks at the way your thoughts about yourself and others do the same thing. Not surprisingly, then, when used together as part of a combined treatment, CBT examines the way your thoughts, behaviors, and emotions influence each other and your overall mental health.

Cognitive therapy was largely developed by Aaron Beck, an American psychiatrist, in the 1960s and 1970s. While doing research on depression, he discovered that people often make errors in their thinking that fuel their mental health problems. Here are some of the common distortions that Beck identified. We're using our own experience with the writing and publishing of *Therapy 101* to illustrate these common distortions:

- **Overgeneralization:** Making broad negative conclusions about life based on limited situations. ("*Therapy 101* wasn't nominated for a Pulitzer Prize; our careers as writers are over.")

- **Minimization and magnification:** Discounting the positive and enlarging the negative. ("All those people who wrote good reviews were just being kind to us, but the one person who wrote that negative review is really going to ruin our careers as writers.")

- **Arbitrary inferences:** Making negative conclusions based on little evidence. ("Those two women at the other table are laughing. They must be laughing at us because they know we're not good writers.")

- **Selective abstraction:** Focusing on one negative detail instead of the larger picture. ("We know *Therapy 101* sold thousands of copies, but it still didn't make the best-sellers lists.")

- **Personalization:** Identifying yourself as the cause of a negative event, whether or not it's true. ("The reason the world is such a mess is because we weren't able to sell enough copies of *Therapy 101*.")

Beck also recognized that people who are depressed and anxious have very pessimistic views about their lives, they underestimate their abilities to cope with problems, and they struggle with repetitive *automatic thoughts*. These are critical thoughts that you frequently think and say to yourself, which sabotage your success and happiness and make you feel sad or anxious. Examples of automatic thoughts might be "I don't deserve anything good happening to me" or "Why bother trying? I'm just going to fail." Thoughts like these can occur consciously or without any awareness that you're thinking them.

Oh. In a January 2000 interview in *The New York Times*, Aaron Beck, one of the cofounders of cognitive therapy, recounted how he was originally trained in the Freudian tradition. As a young psychoanalyst, Beck would make unprompted interpretations about his patients' thoughts and feelings as they lay on his couch. In one early case, he guessed that his patient was nervous because she didn't want to talk to him about her sexual feelings. Her response inspired Beck to create a new type of therapy in which he *asks* his patients how they're feeling instead of making assumptions: "Actually," she replied, "I'm afraid that I'm boring you."

Much of the work in CBT is to help you reevaluate these errors in your thinking and your automatic thoughts. This can be done by "testing" your thoughts using a *thought log*. Your

> *Your success will depend on the amount of work you put into the process.*

therapist will help you look for evidence that supports and contradicts these thoughts, and then he or she will help you create a more balanced thought. For example, if you struggle with anxiety and habitually think to yourself, "Nothing I ever do is good enough," your therapist will ask you for examples of this being true and examples of it not being true from your life. Then, hopefully, you'll be able to come up with a more balanced thought that eases your anxiety, such as "Even though I don't do everything perfectly, I'm still capable of doing most things pretty well."

Overall, CBT is both a very active and interactive process. Throughout your treatment, your therapist will collaborate with you, ask you questions, provide you with feedback, and be an energetic partner in your recovery. However, he or she won't do your work for you. Your success will depend on the amount of work you put into the process. In fact, in CBT, homework is assigned on a weekly basis, and you might be asked to try new behaviors or to keep a record of your thoughts. This is different than many other types of therapy.

CBT therapists often teach their clients new problem-solving and coping methods, such as assertive communication skills, relaxation skills, and social communication skills. Often these skills are taught by means of role-playing during sessions.

For problems like phobias, panic disorder, and obsessive-compulsive disorder, you might also use a behavioral treatment called exposure and response prevention. This process will help you to confront your feared situations in a safe, systematic way, either in real life or in your imagination, and help you realize that you won't be harmed by what you fear.

Cognitive behavioral therapy is effective for treating:

- Anger control problems
- Anorexia
- Antisocial personality disorder
- Attention-deficit/ hyperactivity disorder (ADHD)
- Avoidant personality disorder
- Binge-eating disorder
- Bipolar disorder-related issues
- Body dysmorphic disorder
- Bulimia
- Conversion disorder
- Dependent personality disorder
- Depression
- Dissociative disorders
- Drug and alcohol problems
- Generalized anxiety disorder
- Hypochondriasis
- Impulse control disorders
- Narcissistic personality disorder
- Obsessive-compulsive disorder
- Pain disorder
- Panic disorder
- Paranoid personality disorder
- Phobias
- Post-traumatic stress disorder
- Relationship problems
- Schizoid personality disorder
- Schizotypal personality disorder
- Schizophrenia-related issues
- Sleep disorders
- Social anxiety disorder and social phobia
- Somatization disorder

For more information, visit the websites of:

- The Association for Behavioral and Cognitive Therapies: www.abct.org

- The International Association for Cognitive Psychotherapy: www.cognitivetherapyassociation.org

- The National Association of Cognitive-Behavioral Therapists: www.nacbt.org

Now you try it: *Think of something that's been bothering you lately. Write a sentence or two summarizing the situation and describe how it makes you feel and what your thoughts are about the situation. Then record the evidence that supports how you think about it and the evidence that contradicts how you think about it. Now write a more balanced thought that incorporates all the evidence. Did writing this change the way you feel about the situation that's bothering you?*

INTERPERSONAL THERAPY

Interpersonal therapy (IPT) was developed in the 1980s by Gerald Klerman and Myrna Weissman as a short-term, structured treatment for depression. In some cases, IPT treatment may last for only twelve to sixteen sessions. However, longer treatment is often necessary.

IPT will help you explore how your mental health problems affect your relationships and how those relationships also contribute to your mental health problems. Relationships with romantic partners, family members, friends, and coworkers are all equally important in IPT and need to be examined. It might also be necessary to explore what was happening in your life when your problem developed. But because of the time-limited nature of IPT, little emphasis is placed on exploring your past, beyond how it might currently be affecting your relationships.

IPT focuses on four major causes of relationship problems and, therefore, mental health problems as well. Fights and disagreements between you and your spouse, partner, friends, and so forth, can often cause problems. If they do, your therapist might help you find ways to solve those disputes. The death of a loved one can also lead to issues like depression. If so, your IPT therapist will help you explore your relationship to the person and any feelings you had for him or her. You also might be encouraged to engage in new relationships when the time is right.

Changing roles in your life can also cause difficulties, as it does during divorce, the birth of a child, or getting a promotion at work. If one of your roles has changed , your therapist will help you develop new skills or help you connect with others in order to cope with the

> **Skills versus pills.** In a large 1989 study sponsored by the National Institute of Mental Health, interpersonal therapy and cognitive behavioral therapy were both found to be just as effective for treating mild to moderate depression as some antidepressants, but without the side effects.

situation in a healthier way. Finally, you might be experiencing problems like depression or anxiety because you don't have skills to cope with these issues, in which case, your therapist will teach them to you. For example, assertive communication skills are often taught in IPT as a way to handle many interpersonal situations.

As with the other therapies described in this chapter, IPT is a very interactive process, and you should expect that you and your therapist will rehearse your new skills and role-play your interpersonal interactions in session. You should also expect that you'll be required to do homework outside of your session to reinforce your new skills.

Interpersonal therapy is effective for treating:

- Antisocial personality disorder
- Bipolar disorder-related issues
- Bulimia
- Depression
- Drug and alcohol problems
- Narcissistic personality disorder
- Paranoid personality disorder
- Schizoid personality disorder

For more information, visit the website of:

- The International Society for Interpersonal Psychotherapy:
  www.interpersonalpsychotherapy.org

Now you try it: *If you're currently feeling sad, depressed, or anxious, record five ways in which any of your relationships might be contributing to your problem or five ways in which your problem is causing distress in your relationships.*

RATIONAL EMOTIVE BEHAVIOR THERAPY

Rational emotive behavior therapy (REBT) was created in the 1950s by American psychologist Albert Ellis. It is regarded as one of the first forms of cognitive therapy since it examines how your thoughts affect your emotions and behaviors. According to REBT, *rational thoughts* are healthy thoughts that help you live a more gratifying life, while *irrational thoughts* get in the way of your growth and happiness.

REBT will help you focus on the present moments of your life. It's acknowledged that your self-defeating, irrational thoughts were formed in the past, but the aim of the treatment is to change how those thoughts are affecting you now. As a memory aid, Ellis developed an "ABCDE" approach to mental health. "A" stands for the actions and events in your life, which lead to "C," behavioral and emotional consequences or results. However, what determines how you react to those events is "B," your beliefs. Take, for example, a presidential election ("A," an action). Your reaction to the results of the election, the consequence ("C"), is determined by your belief ("B") about who would make a better leader. If the person you like wins, you're happy. If not, you're disappointed.

To make changes in your life, an REBT therapist will help you dispute ("D") your negative thoughts and rules by looking for evidence that contradicts your irrational beliefs. For example, if you believe, "I'm never going to be any good," your REBT therapist will help you to look for and examine events in your life in which you were successful. An REBT therapist might also help you examine your emotional reactions to a situation, to determine if they're 100 percent accurate. For example, if you're convinced that you're "going to die" if you give a presentation in front of your colleagues, your therapist might help you reexamine that situation and help you to relabel your emotional experience in a more accurate way. Maybe the presentation invokes a certain degree of fear and nervousness that's absolutely normal and understandable. Such relabeling of your emotions can lead to a new experience ("E") of the event.

At the core of REBT is the belief that all humans have the same basic goals. These include being free from suffering, becoming at least moderately happy, and living a fulfilling life. When the results of an activity bring about achieving one of your goals, you try to repeat the activity. When consequences of actions lead to pain or dissatisfaction, you try to avoid those actions in the future. Most people experience minor obstacles when trying to achieve their goals. As a result, they sometimes feel sad or frustrated.

However, according to REBT, some barriers can cause serious problems in your life if you follow strict rules about how your life is supposed to operate. These are often defined by the perfectionist rules of the *shoulds*, *oughts*, and *musts*. For example, if you fail a test and you have a rule that says "I should never fail a test," you're going to react to that situation in a severely negative way. Perhaps you will become depressed, sad, or anxious about the next test. Equally damaging are the irrational beliefs that people have about themselves, such as "I'm never going to be any good." This kind of negative thinking can lead you from one failure to the next throughout your life, until the thought is altered.

> *Negative, irrational thoughts are examined and replaced with healthier, more rational thoughts in REBT.*

Negative, irrational thoughts like these are examined and replaced with healthier, more rational thoughts in REBT. Again, you should expect your therapist to be very interactive with you, and he or

> **Where there's a will...** In a 1988 *Psychology Today* interview with Claire Warga, Albert Ellis recalled how, early in his life, he confronted his own shyness and irrational beliefs about meeting women by forcing himself to talk to over one hundred women he met in his neighborhood park. The result? He got a date—and then he got stood up.

she might even disclose information about him or herself and give personal examples to help you.

You can also expect that you will be encouraged to take risks and engage in behaviors you typically avoid, like speaking in public, in order to extinguish your fears. You'll be assigned homework to do outside of session, which will reinforce the skills you're learning. In addition, REBT utilizes other forms of treatment such as visualization methods, assigning books to read, assertive communication skills training, and role-playing to help you gain the skills you need to create a fulfilling life.

Note that although there is ample evidence to suggest that REBT is an effective treatment and people who use REBT feel better, there is not enough evidence to recommend it for many specific mental health problems.

Rational emotive behavior therapy can be effective for treating:

- Anger

- Anxiety

- Depression

- Problem solving

For more information, visit the website of:

• The Albert Ellis Institute: www.rebt.org

> **Now you try it:** *Pick a problem you're having due to some recent event. Label the event "A" and the consequences "C." Now label your beliefs about the event "B." Can you dispute your beliefs? Label those "D." Now see if it leads to a new way of experiencing the event, "E."*

CHAPTER 2

Exciting, Newer Treatments

These therapies have been developed within the last thirty years and represent some of the best newer treatments available for many different kinds of problems. Two of them, acceptance and commitment therapy and dialectical behavior therapy, are part of the new, so-called third wave of behavioral treatments. Eye movement desensitization and reprocessing uses alternating glances, sounds, or tapping to "dissolve" traumatic memories. Motivational interviewing is a powerful way to treat addictions and change habits. Positive psychology focuses on your strengths and values instead of on your problems. And schema therapy is an extension of cognitive therapy that examines your deep, core beliefs about yourself. Already, they have all improved the ways in which psychotherapy addresses mental health problems.

ACCEPTANCE AND COMMITMENT THERAPY

Acceptance and commitment therapy (ACT) was largely developed by psychologist Steven Hayes in the 1990s. It incorporates elements of behavior therapy and meditation and mindfulness practices, as well as scientific research on how humans learn.

ACT (pronounced "act," as in "do something") is based on the principle that many psychological problems are caused by your efforts to control, avoid, or get rid of undesirable emotions and thoughts. Often, people try to get rid of feelings and thoughts that are sad or anxious just as they would get rid of other things they don't like, such as old clothes. However, as ACT points out, feelings and thoughts can't be controlled. You can't throw them out the same way you get rid of old clothing. In fact, the harder you try to control your thoughts and feelings, the more powerful they become and the longer they stick around. This point can be made by imagining a picture of your favorite cartoon character and then forcing yourself to forget about it. The harder you try not to think about it, the more you actually do. The same is true for your thoughts and emotions, according to ACT.

Many people are taught by their parents or society that sad and anxious thoughts or emotions are "bad," "negative," or "undesirable." Ultimately, these beliefs become rules by which you live your life. Then, when sadness or anxiety appears, you do your best to suppress the emotion, avoid it, or control it. To do this, you might try many different ent methods. For example, you can try not to think about how situations affect you, you can refuse to discuss your feelings, or maybe you use drugs and alcohol to help you forget. Unfortunately, however, these coping

> **The harder you try to control your thoughts and feelings, the more powerful they become.**

> **Necessity is the mother of invention.** In a 2006 *Time* magazine interview, ACT founder Steven Hayes admitted that he himself once struggled with severe panic disorder that almost ended his teaching career as a university professor. Luckily, he eventually overcame the problem but only after he created his own way of treating it.

strategies only make your situation worse. Either they interfere with your relationships or they cause you to become more anxious and depressed.

One of your initial tasks in ACT is to figure out all the strategies you've used to cope with your problems. Your ACT therapist will acknowledge that you've worked very hard at solving your problems in the best ways you knew how and that you've come for treatment only after you've exhausted all your other options. After exploring your unsuccessful attempts to handle your problem, you'll be encouraged to acknowledge the fact that your coping strategies don't work. In ACT, this acknowledgement is called *creative hopelessness*, and its purpose is to make you receptive to new, unexplored possibilities.

To make changes in your life, your ACT therapist will help you explore your personal values. This is an important step because it steers your treatment toward a genuine purpose. ACT's ultimate goal isn't to eliminate all the pain in your life. This would be impossible. The goal is to make your life more meaningful and fulfilling, while accepting the fact that sometimes life also includes sadness and anxiety.

One of the initial steps toward change is to develop skills of self-observation. This means that you'll be asked to pay attention to how your thoughts and feelings affect each other in the present moment. ACT places a large emphasis on the here and now of life. To become better aware of this, you might be instructed in some form of meditation that will help you focus on the present moment. Next, your

ACT therapist will help you learn to *defuse* from your thoughts. This means that you'll be taught how to observe your self-critical thoughts without becoming entangled in them. These skills often include watching thoughts float past in your imagination and learning to treat your mind as a separate entity that produces thoughts without your control. In a similar way, you'll also learn how to accept your sad and anxious thoughts without trying to control or avoid them.

Finally, your ACT therapist will also help you explore the steps that need to be taken in order to live a more fulfilling life, based on your values, and to help you overcome obstacles that stand in the way of those achievements.

Acceptance and commitment therapy is effective for treating:

- Anxiety
- Pain disorders
- Panic disorder
- Phobias
- Post-traumatic stress disorder
- Schizophrenia-related issues

For more information, visit the ACT website at:

- www.contextualpsychology.org/act

Now you try it: *Write a list of the things in life that you value (for example, family, work, education, and fun). Next, estimate on a scale of 1 to 10 how close you are to fulfilling those values in your life. Now, for each one you're not fulfilling, write three specific ways in which you can bring more of those values into your life.*

DIALECTICAL BEHAVIOR THERAPY

Dialectical behavior therapy (DBT), developed by psychologist Marsha Linehan, was created in the early 1990s for people suffering with overwhelming emotions and borderline personality disorder. More recently, the treatment has also been successful at treating other problems, too, like some eating disorders.

DBT is a form of cognitive behavioral therapy. Both types of treatment examine the way your thoughts, feelings, and behaviors interact and affect each other. However, a therapist using DBT is especially interested in how your thoughts can create disruptive behaviors and emotions that interfere with your life and relationships. After examining these interactions, your DBT therapist will help you modify those thoughts, feelings, and behaviors, using different types of skills training.

One of the initial goals of the treatment is to make sure that you're safe. Some people, especially those struggling with borderline personality disorder, engage in suicidal and self-harming behaviors, such as cutting and self-mutilation. One of the most important goals of DBT is to help you control and eliminate these behaviors, if they're a problem for you. You'll also be provided with specific sets of skills to help you solve problems, improve your relationships, improve your control of your behaviors and emotions, and help you tolerate emotional discomfort.

DBT also aims to help you reduce painful symptoms that arise because of trauma, since so many people with overwhelming emotions and borderline personality disorder have also been the victims of some type of abuse, especially sexual abuse. This part of the treatment might involve helping you safely and systematically confront feared situations that you're currently avoiding, like making new friends or dating. Your

> **Om.** In her 1993 book *Cognitive-Behavioral Treatment of Borderline Personality Disorder*, Marsha Linehan writes that her treatment's emphasis on mindfulness skills and acceptance was largely influenced by her own practice of Zen meditation.

DBT therapist might also require you to join a support group therapy program, along with other people who are receiving DBT treatment.

DBT is largely influenced by Zen Buddhism, which emphasizes the acceptance of contradictory thoughts at the same time. The term "dialectic" refers to the examination of contradictory thoughts and behaviors that takes place in DBT. For example, one of the fundamental techniques of the treatment is to teach you how to accept yourself, with all of your problems, while simultaneously acknowledging that you need to make some basic changes if your life is going to improve.

Acceptance and change are two key concepts that are repeatedly balanced in DBT. Mindfulness skills based on Buddhist meditation are also taught. These skills can help you observe your actions, thoughts, emotions, and environment without making any judgmental responses.

Overall, DBT is a very active treatment. For it to be effective, you will be expected to implement and practice all of these new skills in your life outside of the therapy office. That's where most of the improvements in your life will take place. Initially, your DBT therapist may require you to agree on the goals of the treatment, especially the goals of not engaging in suicidal behaviors, self-harm, or other things that interfere with the treatment process. And as previously stated, you'll also be expected to participate in any other individual therapy or group therapy sessions that your DBT therapist requires.

Dialectical behavior therapy is effective for treating:

- Attention-deficit/ hyperactivity disorder (ADHD)

- Binge-eating disorder

- Borderline personality disorder

- Bulimia

- Paranoid personality disorder

- Problems related to overwhelming emotions

For more information, visit the websites of:

- The Behavioral Research and Therapy Clinics: www.brtc.psych. washington.edu

- The Association for Behavioral and Cognitive Therapies: www.abct.org

Now you try it: *Learning to tolerate and soothe your painful emotions is a key element of DBT. Make a list of ways that you can soothe yourself using all of your senses, such as listening to calming music, taking a warm bath, looking at some peaceful scenery, or eating a good meal. Then, the next time you're feeling overwhelmed by your emotions, try one of your ideas.*

EYE MOVEMENT DESENSITIZATION AND REPROCESSING

Eye movement desensitization and reprocessing (EMDR) was created by psychologist Francine Shapiro in the 1980s to help people who had experienced traumas. However, there is now research to support the claim that EMDR successfully treats other mental health problems as well.

EMDR was once publicized in the media as a one-time cure for trauma. Yet, even the founder of the treatment says that this is not an accurate statement. EMDR, like other treatments for trauma, can take weeks, months, or years to reduce your symptoms, depending on the severity of your trauma, and it doesn't work for everyone.

To someone who is unfamiliar with the treatment, the methods used in EMDR might look very strange when compared to other talk-based therapies. To put it simply, in EMDR you'll be asked to recall a memory that sums up your traumatic event. Then you'll be told to focus on your psychotherapist's fingers as he or she moves them from right to left, in a steady rhythm, for approximately thirty seconds at a time. Then the process is repeated. Although this may seem odd, moving your eyes from side to side does seem to produce a calming effect. The treatment also works through a process called *desensitizing*, which means that the pain associated with your memory decreases as you continuously recall the image throughout the treatment.

Another supporting theory suggests that EMDR helps your brain to process disturbing information. Memories of a trauma are usually so upsetting that people don't want to think about them, and so the information remains unprocessed. In this raw form, the memory can be very distressing, especially if it makes you think that you're to blame for what happened. EMDR supporters believe that desensitization of

Clinician, heal thyself. The first "patient" of Francine Shapiro's EMDR treatment was herself. One day, while out for a walk, she noticed that her distressing thoughts were disappearing after her eyes moved in a side-to-side fashion. She then took the technique back to her research center and found that it worked for others as well.

the memory allows the brain to process the traumatizing information and "file it away."

In actuality, the treatment is more involved than simply watching your psychotherapist's fingers move back and forth. In the initial stages, your therapist will help you learn to relax and imagine a "safe place" for yourself, just in case the process of recalling the trauma becomes too overwhelming. Your EMDR therapist will also help you select an image from the trauma that encapsulates your experience and then help you explore how that memory makes you think of yourself. In the next phase, you'll hold that snapshot in your memory for a few seconds and then watch the fingers of your therapist move from side to side. But once the movement starts, you'll be instructed to let that memory go and just pay attention to other images and feelings that arise.

After every set of finger movements, you'll be asked to describe the memories and feelings that came up for you. Then the movements begin again. Periodically, your EMDR therapist will ask you about the original memory of the trauma. The process continues until your emotional reaction to that memory is minimally disturbing. Finally, in the last stages of treatment, your EMDR therapist will help you implant a positive thought about yourself instead of the painful one that resulted from the trauma.

In addition to using side-to-side eye movements, this treatment is also effective when using other alternating techniques, such as tapping your left and right knees or snapping your fingers near your left and right ears.

Another treatment similar to EMDR is the *eye movement technique* (EMT). EMT is a simpler technique that also uses side-to-side eye movements to reduce the anxiety of traumatic memories. You follow your therapist's finger, focus on points on the wall, tap alternating knees, or close your eyes and move them back and forth. However, unlike EMDR, EMT requires you to hold on to the disturbing memory while you're moving your eyes. The result is that the memory breaks up and becomes harder to recall, thereby reducing the anxiety related to the memory.

EMDR is effective for treating:

- Body dysmorphic disorder
- Dissociative disorders
- Post-traumatic stress disorder

For more information, visit the websites of:

- The EMDR Institute, Inc.: www.emdr.com
- The EMDR International Association: www.emdria.org

Now you try it: *Think of a slightly distressing memory, like the frustration of driving in heavy traffic (don't pick a memory that's too emotional or overwhelming). Now close your eyes, hold on to that memory, and move your eyes side to side for about thirty seconds. Notice if the memory has lost some of its emotional sting. Repeat if necessary.*

MOTIVATIONAL INTERVIEWING AND THE STAGES OF CHANGE MODEL

Motivational interviewing is a therapeutic technique that's often used to change unhealthy behaviors such as alcohol and drug use, poor diet, and a lack of exercise. It was developed by psychologist William Miller in the 1980s and later expanded upon with the help of psychologist Stephen Rollnick.

At the heart of motivational interviewing is the belief that people fail to make changes in their lives because they feel conflicted about making those changes. Often, even an unhealthy behavior like drinking too much alcohol might have some desirable effects, like making a person feel "more relaxed" or "more accepted by others."

This ambivalence between the benefits of changing versus the benefits of not changing is the target of treatment in motivational interviewing. A therapist using this technique will help you explore your ambivalence and the discrepancy between what you want and what's getting in your way. This process might include identifying your values, goals, and the life you'd like to create, while also looking at how your present behaviors interfere with those plans.

Motivational interviewing is a client-centered and collaborative process, meaning it is you who directs the movement of the treatment. A therapist using this technique often plays the role of an empathic, interested listener who repeats what you say in order to make sure he or she understands you correctly and to allow you to really hear what you're saying. A therapist using motivational interviewing will help you stay on the topic of changing a habit, but he or she will not tell you what or how to do it. Instead, your therapist might provide you with a menu of change options, if you ask for suggestions, and then allow you to choose what's best for you.

Underlying motivational interviewing is the belief that you are solely responsible for making and sustaining changes in your own life. As such, *lasting* changes cannot be imposed upon you by someone else, such as your therapist. You will change a behavior in your life, and maintain that change, only when the motivation to do so comes from within yourself.

The motivation to make changes is considered to be a quality that can be increased, rather than being thought of as a stable personality trait. For example, a person with diabetes might originally think that it's impossible to change his diet because he thinks of himself as a person who's stuck in his ways. But with the help of motivational interviewing, he might commit to making some type of small change and therefore increase his motivation to make even more changes in the future.

A therapist using motivational interviewing will avoid arguing with you or trying to persuade you about when or how to make changes in your life. Instead, the therapist will allow you to make those decisions yourself. It's understood that people change at different rates and in different ways, and rarely do they completely change something in their lives overnight.

In order to guide you through your own process of change, a therapist using motivational interviewing will also use the *stages of change model*. The stages of change model, developed by psychologists James Prochaska and Carlo DiClemente, says that people move through five stages when they're changing habits and behaviors in their lives, rather than going directly from doing something to not doing something.

During the first stage, *pre-contemplation*, you don't consider your behavior to be a problem and you aren't even thinking about changing it. In the second stage, *contemplation*, you're aware that your behavior is causing some problems in your life. You're also willing to consider

> **If at first you don't succeed…** There are many schemes out there that promise a quick fix to change your old habits. Most of them won't work if you don't already want to change in the first place. Changing any habit takes a lot of practice, motivation, compassion for yourself, and the conviction to keep trying if you don't succeed on the first attempt.

making changes, weighing the pros and cons of change, and you're willing to talk about making changes, but you haven't committed to taking action yet. During the third stage, *preparation*, you've committed to changing your behavior within the next thirty days and you've made a plan to change. In the fourth stage, *action*, you're participating in making those changes, and in the fifth stage, *maintenance*, you're actively taking steps to maintain those changes in your life.

During your treatment using motivational interviewing, you will be asked how confident you are on a scale of 0 to 10 that you can make the desired changes in your life, and what actions or type of motivation it would take to move you along in the stages of change, closer to taking action.

Motivational interviewing is effective for:

- Alcohol and drug problems

- Changing dietary habits

- Increasing physical exercise

- Changing unwanted behaviors and habits

For more information visit the website of:

• Motivational Interviewing Resources:
  www.motivationalinterview.org

Now you try it: *Using the description of the stages of change model, pick a behavior that you'd like to change. Identify what stage of change you're in. Now record some thoughts about what it would take to move you into the "action" phase.*

POSITIVE PSYCHOLOGY

Positive psychology was largely created by psychologists Martin Seligman, Christopher Peterson, Mihaly Csikszentmihalyi, and C. R. Snyder around the year 2000. As you might have guessed, positive psychology focuses on your strengths and virtues. It's meant to complement and balance other types of psychotherapy that largely focus on the treatment of your problems and deficits.

The goals of positive psychology include helping you create a happier, more fulfilling life and reaching your greatest potential. Equally important are the goals of focusing on your positive strengths to help you maintain your psychological health, and possibly prevent mental health problems like depression and anxiety, as well as to maintain your physical health, and possibly prevent problems such as job burnout.

In an attempt to create a cross-cultural list of virtues, one group of positive psychologists studied the values of ancient philosophies from both Asia and the West. Among the common virtues found were wisdom, courage, humanity, justice, temperance, and transcendence, which refers to beliefs and actions that help to explain the meaning of life.

By helping you explore qualities such as these, a therapist using positive psychology hopes to help you build strengths and skills, such as creativity, hope, love, bravery, fairness, humor, kindness, forgiveness,

☺ In a January 2005 cover story in *Time* magazine, Seligman and other positive psychologists discussed the three key elements of long-lasting happiness: "getting more pleasure out of life, becoming more engaged in what you do, and finding ways of making your life feel more meaningful."

gratitude, and authenticity. There's some evidence that cultivating these strengths may be good for you in many ways, and qualities such as hope, altruism, and optimism can improve both your physical and mental health. In addition, happiness and the expression of positive emotions have been associated with longer, healthier, and more fulfilling lives.

Studies of positive psychology techniques have demonstrated that simple treatment exercises can have dramatic effects. A 2005 study by Seligman and colleagues found that activities such as utilizing your strengths on a daily basis, delivering a letter to thank someone, and recording three good things that happened to you each day can increase your happiness and decrease symptoms of depression for as long as six months. Other techniques used in positive psychology often include writing, meditation, and getting out into nature.

Positive psychology is effective for:

- Treating depression-related symptoms
- Treating low levels of happiness
- Self-growth

For more information, visit the website of:

- The Positive Psychology Center: www.ppc.sas.upenn.edu

Now you try it: *At the end of every day for the next two weeks, write down three good things that happened to you, and notice if you feel any better because of it. Repeat as necessary.*

SCHEMA THERAPY

Schema therapy, developed by psychologist Jeffrey Young in the 1990s, can help you examine the repetitive and dysfunctional patterns of thoughts and relationships that commonly interfere with your life. A *schema* is a strongly held positive or negative belief that you have about yourself, which you think is true, even if it causes harm or difficulties in your life.

Here are a few common, problematic schemas that often develop in childhood and persist into adulthood, illustrated with examples:

- **Abandonment or instability**: Being frequently scared of relationships ending. ("I don't care how well my relationship is going right now, I know my partner will eventually leave me.")

- **Defectiveness or shame**: The belief that you're defective in some way and therefore undeserving of being loved or cared for by anyone. ("I'm no good, ugly, and unworthy of anyone's love.")

- **Vulnerability to harm or illness**: The belief that you're exceptionally at risk for getting hurt or contracting some type of illness. ("I can't take chances in life or try new things because I might get hurt.")

- **Failure:** The belief that you've never succeeded, nor can you ever succeed, no matter what the task. ("Why even bother trying? I'm never going to have a successful relationship.")

- **Self-sacrifice**: The belief, or experience, that you willingly give up your own needs in order to meet someone else's needs. ("It's not important for me to be happy; it's more important that I take care of everyone else.")

- **Approval-seeking or recognition-seeking**: The belief that you constantly have to gain the appreciation and support of others in order to have a sense of valid self-worth. ("If my friends don't like what I'm wearing, I'll have to put on something different.")

- **Emotional inhibition**: The belief that you should stop yourself from saying, doing, or feeling certain things because they might offend someone else. ("I shouldn't feel happy about my successes, because it might make my friends feel uncomfortable.")

- **Unrelenting standards or excessive criticism**: The belief that you should set excessively high goals for yourself that are often impossible to meet or damaging to your life. ("I have to be the best spouse and best employee, who never makes any mistakes.")

The overall goals of schema therapy are to reduce the strengths of your negative schemas, to develop healthier thoughts and feelings about yourself, and to help you engage in healthier behaviors.

A schema is a strongly held belief that you have about yourself, which you think is true, even if it causes harm or difficulties in your life.

Schema therapy generally includes two stages of treatment, starting with an exploratory stage. In this beginning phase, you and your therapist

> **A chip off the old block.** Schemas also play an important role in cognitive behavioral therapy (CBT), developed by psychiatrist Aaron Beck. Not surprisingly, Jeffrey Young, the creator of schema therapy, was a student of Beck's at the University of Pennsylvania.

will examine your problems and identify the schemas that have been interfering with your life. This may include having you fill out a detailed questionnaire of some common schema problems. Your schema therapist will also help you understand how your early childhood experiences created those beliefs, help you recognize any feelings associated with those beliefs, and assist you in identifying how you've coped with those distressing thoughts and feelings in the past.

Generally, people deal with schema problems in three different ways. They avoid their problems, they maintain their problems, or they overcompensate and do the exact opposite of what their schemas tell them to do. Unfortunately, all of these actions serve only to make the schema stronger and the associated problems worse.

The second phase of treatment focuses on changing the schema and its related behaviors. This includes examining the evidence in your life that supports and refutes your schema. Usually, more evidence can be found to disprove your negative thoughts about yourself than can be found to support them. So, part of treatment also involves creating new, positive thoughts about yourself based on the new evidence.

Schema therapy will also help you get in touch with any childhood pain that might have been caused by these negative thoughts. Part of your treatment might include the use of imagination exercises to heal those old wounds. You'll also investigate how your schemas affect your current relationships, including your relationship with your therapist. Instead of relying on dysfunctional methods of coping with your schema, your schema therapist will help you initiate healthier behavioral changes to counteract your old schema patterns. This might include learning new communication skills and relaxation skills, which you'll need to practice in your daily life by doing your homework.

Schema therapy can be effective for treating:

- Borderline personality disorder
- Other personality disorders
- Relationship problems
- Repetitive problems in your life that share similar themes

For more information, visit the website of:

- The Schema Therapy Institute: www.schematherapy.com

> **Now you try it:** *Think of five relationship problems you've had with people who are important to you in some way. Can you identify any common threads between the problems, either in the way you treated them or in the way they treated you? How would you summarize that problem, and what needs to be changed?*

CHAPTER 3

Humanistic Treatments

The following treatments stem from the humanistic school of therapy created by Abraham Maslow and Carl Rogers in the 1940s. When these treatments were created, they caused a controversy in the world of psychotherapy. At the time, the field was dominated by traditional Freudian psychoanalysis in which the doctor was the expert and the patient did most of the talking. In humanistic therapy, the client is viewed as the expert on his or her own problem and the treatment process is very interactive, with the client leading the process and making treatment decisions, such as when and how often to meet.

In this chapter you'll learn about the most common forms of humanistic treatments. Client-centered therapy was the original humanistic therapy created by Rogers in the 1940s. Existential psychotherapy was heavily influenced by the thinking of nineteenth-century existential philosophy. Gestalt therapy examines the total nature of who you are. Reality therapy takes the radical position that you create your own problems. Solution-focused therapy emphasizes what you can do about your problems. And transpersonal therapy focuses on the spiritual nature of human existence.

The positive impact of humanistic treatments on the field of psychotherapy has been great. All of these treatments can help you cope with general problems of living, aid your self-growth, and give you insight about who you are. However, because of the unspecific form and protocol of these treatments, there is little research to validate their use for specific problems, such as anxiety, phobias, or depression, which you should consider when choosing one of these treatments.

CLIENT-CENTERED THERAPY/ PERSON-CENTERED THERAPY

Client-centered therapy, or *person-centered therapy,* was developed by psychologist Carl Rogers in the 1940s. Client-centered therapy is a nondirective form of treatment, meaning that your therapist will follow your lead in session and regard you as the expert on your own experience. As such, your therapist's job will be to follow the direction that you want to go in, instead of leading you toward some purpose or goal of treatment. Your client-centered therapist trusts that you will speak naturally about what you need to do in the therapy session, without his or her guidance, and eventually you will figure out the key to your problem. He or she also trusts that you know how often you need to come in for treatment and for how long a period of time. So you will also make these decisions.

Client-centered therapy takes an optimistic view of the human experience. One of the foundations of the therapy is that people naturally move toward their own growth and the fulfillment of their true potential in life. Mental health problems occur when you develop a rigid way of viewing yourself and the world, and, therefore, stop growing. The aim of a client-centered therapist is to provide you with a supportive environment in which you can figure out your problem and continue growing toward self-fulfillment, or *self-actualization.*

In order to facilitate this growth, your client-centered therapist will seek to embody three characteristics: to be genuine, to show you unconditional positive regard, and to be sincerely empathetic. To be *genuine* means that your psychotherapist will behave as a real person who doesn't act in a phony or authoritarian way. *Unconditional positive regard* means that your therapist should treat you in a completely nonjudgmental way and accept whatever you do or say no matter what, even if your opinion differs greatly from his or her own opinion. *Empathy*

And the prize goes to... Considered by many to be one of the most influential psychologists of the twentieth century, Carl Rogers was nominated for the 1987 Nobel Peace Prize for coordinating peace talks in the Soviet Union, South Africa, and Central America. Unfortunately, he did not win.

requires your therapist to act and respond to you in a genuine, warm, and caring way and to check in with you in order to verify that he or she has understood you correctly.

By using these techniques, your client-centered therapist seeks to help you in a number of ways. It's hoped that you will improve your self-esteem, develop a sense of control that comes from within yourself rather than from some outside source, become more open to experiencing new possibilities in your life, and develop more flexible coping styles and attitudes.

Traditionally, client-centered therapy treats all patients the same regardless of the presenting problem. It's also common that a client-centered therapist won't take a history of your problem and won't put a focus on your diagnosis. Again, the treatment is more concerned with you as a whole person rather than just with your problems.

Client-centered therapy is effective for:

• Self-growth and personal insight

For more information, visit the website of:

• The Association for Humanistic Psychology:
www.ahpweb.org

Now you try it: *How would your life look different if you were self-actualized or self-fulfilled? Write a story describing your new life. Now try to identify the steps you'll have to take to get there.*

EXISTENTIAL PSYCHOTHERAPY

Existential psychotherapy took hold in Europe after the destruction caused by World War II, and later it became popular in the United States. Among its developers were psychologist Rollo May, psychiatrist Irvin Yalom, and psychiatrist Victor Frankl. More so than other forms of psychotherapy, *existential psychotherapy* is largely influenced by philosophy, especially the thoughts of early European existentialists such as Kierkegaard, Nietzsche, and Heidegger.

The name of the psychotherapy comes from the same root as the word "exist." This form of treatment, therefore, focuses on your existence and how it influences your view of life and the world. The aim of existential psychotherapy is to examine you as a whole person, rather than as a composite of impulses. It's built on the principle that there is no one truth to explain history or life, because each person's view of the world is unique. There is no standard technique used in existential psychotherapy; instead, it offers a set of guidelines for looking at yourself and your problems in a unique way.

Existential psychotherapy emphasizes living a fuller, more meaningful life despite the fact that many situations in modern society can feel depressing and without substance. The task is to examine the way you give meaning to the elements of your life, such as love, illness, relationships, and your personal self. According to existential psychotherapy, anxiety problems develop when you are confronted with large issues that threaten you. Typically, the most disturbing

> *There is no one truth to explain history or life, because each person's view of the world is unique.*

> **Strength of the human spirit.** Despite his own suffering and the murder of his family in the Nazi concentration camps of World War II, existential psychiatrist Victor Frankl was able to find a purpose in his life and hope for mankind, which he writes about in *Man's Search for Meaning*.

issues are death, isolation, a loss of meaning, and freedom (yes, even freedom can cause anxiety).

The first three issues all seem like obvious ones with which to be concerned. However, freedom requires you to take responsibility for your actions and it requires you to make choices that can change your world and possibly affect others. This responsibility frequently makes people nervous. Therefore, part of a treatment plan might be to help you take responsibility for making changes that have been avoided, to learn to tolerate being alone, and to find meaning in life by participating in new activities.

Existential psychotherapy does share some similarities with psychoanalysis, such as the belief in unconscious and conscious thoughts that can contribute to anxiety. Part of the goal of existential psychotherapy is to uncover those thoughts and to examine how they're impeding your life. However, existential psychotherapy is more concerned with exploring your present problem and future goals, rather than uncovering the past roots of your problem, as you would do in psychoanalysis.

Existential psychology is effective for:

- Self-growth and personal insight

For more information, visit the website of:

- The International Society for Existential Psychology and
  Psychotherapy: www.existentialpsychology.org

> **Now you try it:** *What are your thoughts and feelings about the existential concepts of death, isolation, loss of meaning, and freedom? Record your ideas and how they might be influencing your life.*

GESTALT THERAPY

The form of gestalt therapy popular today was largely created in the 1950s and 1960s by psychiatrist Frederick "Fritz" Perls and his wife Laura Perls, a psychologist.

The word "gestalt" means a whole that is greater than the sum of its individual parts. Similarly, *gestalt therapy* views you as a whole being who's inseparable from your surroundings, friends, family, memories, or past. Thus, in order to understand your problem, your gestalt therapist must help you understand all of those elements and how they interact in your life.

However, despite the connection you have with your past, gestalt therapy is primarily concerned with the here and now. The goal of the treatment is to help you become more fully aware of what's happening to you in the present moment. By gaining this awareness, and making responsible decisions for your life based on that awareness, you can become healthier. To achieve this, your gestalt therapist might engage you in some very interactive experiences to highlight new ways of thinking, feeling, and acting.

For example, one technique involves having you talk to an empty chair in the room, as if you were talking to someone from your life with whom you have difficulty communicating. Talking to the empty chair allows you to say all the things that you always wanted to—but never did. Alternatively, you might write a letter to that person (which is never sent), and then write a response letter back from that person, imagining what he or she would say to you in return.

In other cases, you might use visualization techniques to imagine new reactions to troubling situations, or your gestalt therapist might help you focus your attention on your body posture and breathing habits, in order to understand how your body is responding to how you are feeling. However, despite these commonly used techniques, there

---

Out of sight, out of mind? Early in their careers, both Fritz and Laura Perls worked as traditional Freudian psychoanalysts. This meant they sat out of sight, behind their patients, who would lie on a couch while talking. In a 1978 interview in the *Gestalt Journal*, Laura later admitted that although Fritz usually smoked up to four packs of cigarettes a day while sitting behind his patients, she had preferred to knit.

---

is no official form of gestalt therapy. Rather, there's a common philosophy that guides the treatment and places an emphasis on helping you experiment with whatever means are necessary to move you toward health and wholeness.

Because this form of treatment is so interactive, it's very important that you and your gestalt therapist develop a trusting, cooperative, and therapeutic relationship. Relationships in general are a very important focus of gestalt psychotherapy, but in session, it's exceptionally important that you trust your therapist enough to engage in experimentation. To foster this trust, a gestalt therapist might share stories from his or her own life to illustrate a point or to help you when you're struggling. In contrast, your gestalt therapist might also openly challenge your stories and reported feelings. But even this is done with the best of intentions. This type of challenge can help reveal an underlying thought, emotion, or behavior of which you are not aware. It can also help you understand how you affect other people. Or it can help you learn to react to a challenge in a new, healthier way.

Other basic principles of gestalt therapy include the belief that people naturally seek balance in their lives, *homeostasis*, and want to improve their health. However, people sometimes get stuck using old habits that worked in the past but no longer help in the present. For example, when you were a child, maybe you tried to please everyone to get attention, but now that you are an adult, that same strategy leads only to continual emotional and physical exhaustion. In gestalt therapy, you would experiment with new, healthier ways of dealing with those situations. Gestalt therapy is also similar to existential psychotherapy in that it's interested in how you make sense of some of the larger issues in life, such as death, freedom, and isolation.

Gestalt therapy is effective for:

- Self-growth and personal insight

For more information, visit the websites of:

- The Association for the Advancement of Gestalt Therapy: www.aagt.org

- The Gestalt Therapy Network: www.gestalttherapy.net

Now you try it: *Pick a person in your life with whom you've had a difficult relationship. Write a letter to that person (with no intention of ever sending it), letting that person know how he or she made you feel and affected your life. Now, pretend to respond for that person and write a letter back to yourself, writing what you think he or she would really say to you. Then write a letter back to yourself saying what you would hope he or she would say to you.*

REALITY THERAPY

Reality therapy, also known as *choice theory*, is a treatment created by psychiatrist William Glasser in the 1960s. Reality therapy is based on the radical idea that each person is solely responsible for creating and treating their own mental health problems. The theory rejects the medical model of mental illness, which holds that problems like depression are due to chemical imbalances in the brain. A therapist using reality therapy would say that you aren't being "depressed" by something outside of yourself, but rather you are choosing to "depress" yourself. According to reality therapy, this holds true for most mental health issues like anxiety, depression, phobias, addiction, anger, and even schizophrenia. Only problems such as Alzheimer's dementia or Huntington's disease can be explained by brain dysfunctions.

Reality therapy is based on the premise that you become unhappy when you make poor decisions to fulfill one of your basic human needs for survival, power, freedom, fun, or love and belonging. Of all of these needs, love and belonging are the most important. When you are able to get these needs met in a responsible way, you will have adopted a *success identity*. But when your needs are not met, or when they are met in an unhealthy way, you have adopted a *failure identity*.

According to the theory, unsatisfying relationships or feelings of being are disconnected from others are probably at the core of most

---

Excuse me, Mr. Einstein? Apparently, even Albert Einstein wasn't quite sure what to make of the nature of reality when he supposedly uttered this quote: "Reality is merely an illusion, albeit a very persistent one."

---

of your mental health issues. When a person with a failure identity feels unsatisfied or disconnected from others, he or she often makes unsuccessful attempts to blame, change, or control other people. For example, a

> *Reality therapy helps you determine what you can do right now to improve your life.*

woman in an unsatisfying relationship might consciously or unconsciously depress herself for a number of reasons, including to get help from others (such as her family members) without having to ask for it, to avoid activities she doesn't want to do or is scared of doing (like acting more assertively), or to avoid getting angry (which many people were taught to avoid doing as children).

Treatment in reality therapy includes looking at your *total behavior*, that is, your actions, thoughts, emotions, and physiology, which all work together in every choice you make. In order to create a success identity, a reality therapist will focus on helping you learn to make better choices in your actions and thoughts, which are easier to control than your emotions and physiology (which often follow your actions and thoughts).

Reality therapy is also a present-focused treatment, meaning it helps you determine what you can do right now to improve your life. Understanding why your problem developed is not as important as learning how you can change your life at the present moment. Your reality therapist will help you make a plan to regain control of your life, teach you skills that you might need, and help you develop more satisfying relationships, either with people who are already in your life or with new people.

Reality therapy is effective for:

- Self-growth and personal insight

For more information visit the website of:

- The William Glasser Institute: www.wglasser.com

> **Now you try it:** *Think about the decisions you've made in your life to fulfill your needs for survival, power, freedom, fun, or love and belonging. How have they turned out? Well or not so well? Record some of your ideas about how you can get these needs fulfilled in a more responsible way and create a success identity.*

SOLUTION-FOCUSED THERAPY

Solution-focused therapy was developed in the 1980s by psychologists Steve de Shazer and Insoo Kim Berg. It is a practical, brief form of treatment, usually lasting five to eight sessions, and unlike many other forms of therapy it focuses on what's going right in your life instead of focusing on what's going wrong.

An initial session of solution-focused therapy might begin with a question like "What do you hope to get out of therapy?" The purpose of this question, as well as the treatment, is to move your life toward some goal that you value. Little to no time will be spent taking a detailed history of your problem, analyzing its origins, or giving you a diagnosis. Solution-focused therapy works under the belief that you don't need insight into your problem in order to solve it.

Solution-focused therapy is a collaborative process. You can expect your therapist to be encouraging and to help you remember your past accomplishments, but, ultimately, it is you who will guide the treatment. With the help of your therapist, you will decide what needs to be changed in your life and the steps necessary to bring about that change. Sometimes, it will be helpful to explore other aspects of your life that are already going well and to apply those skills to the more problematic areas. For example, if you're successful at your job but experience problems in your relationships, maybe some of your work skills could help you, such as persistence, timeliness, and paying attention to details.

To guide you in your process, solution-focused therapists often ask a series of common questions. Initially, you might be asked an *exception question* such as "Are there any times when you don't have this problem, even for a short amount of time? What's different? What

> *Solution-focused therapy works under the belief that you don't need insight into your problem in order to solve it.*

Solving problems at work, too. With its practical, problem-solving approach, and its track record of success, solution-focused therapy has also been applied to the world of business. Its methods are now used to facilitate managerial decision making, executive coaching, and project management.

conditions would be necessary to do this again?" One of the underlying beliefs of solution-focused therapy is that people are often more resourceful and capable of dealing with their problems then they give themselves credit for, so they have to be reminded of their successes and skills. Hopefully, the exception question will help you remember times when you were able to cope with your problem in a healthier way and to identify the skills you used then, which you can now use again.

Another common question is the *miracle question*: "Suppose in the middle of the night a miracle occurred and all of the problems that brought you into therapy had been solved. When you woke up in the morning, what would you notice as being different? How would others recognize that your life had changed? Specifically, what would be different about you?" The purpose of this question is to identify the detailed ways in which you want your daily life to improve. To simply say "I want to feel better" or "I want my life to be easier" is too vague. This question will help you think of the observable ways in which you want your life to improve, such as "I'll have more energy to do things" or "my wife and I will talk more often." By clarifying your goals this way, you'll be able to more easily recognize when they've been accomplished.

Each week when you return to treatment, your therapist might begin the session with a question like "What's changed this week?" or "What's been better?" If your situation has improved, your therapist will help you identify the progress you're making toward your goals, what happened, how other people have noticed or responded, what the effect has been on your life, and how that progress might continue into the future. If your situation hasn't improved or if it's worsened, your therapist will be interested in the skills you used to cope with your problems.

Throughout the treatment, your solution-focused therapist will also use *scaling questions* to gauge your progress toward reaching your goals. For example, he or she might ask you, "On a scale of 1 to 10, with 10 being the accomplishment of your goal and 1 being the furthest point from your goal, where are you right now?" or "On a scale of 1 to 10, how confident are you that you can change your life for the better today?" Again, questions like these are designed to help you recognize the progress you're making toward achieving your goals and improving your life.

Solution-focused therapy might be effective for:

- Changing problematic behaviors in adults and adolescents
- Reducing mild to moderate depression
- Self-growth and personal insight

For more information visit the website of:

- The Brief Family Therapy Center: www.brief-therapy.org

Now you try it: *Use the miracle question to identify the specific ways in which you'd like your life to change: "Suppose in the middle of the night a miracle occurred and all of your problems had been solved. When you woke up in the morning, what would you notice as being different? How would others recognize that your life had changed? What specifically would be different about you?" Now create a plan of specific steps to move your life in that direction.*

TRANSPERSONAL PSYCHOLOGY

Transpersonal psychology is a treatment that combines psychotherapy with spiritual principles and beliefs. It is a school of thought that can trace its roots back to the early development of psychology and to such figures as William James and Carl Jung, among others, who were interested in the influence of spiritual experiences. However, this treatment is different than religious counseling, which emphasizes the doctrine of one particular faith. A transpersonal psychologist will often borrow spiritual and religious teachings from many faiths, including Buddhism, Christianity, Judaism, Sufism, Hinduism, and even agnosticism.

Transpersonal means to go beyond individual experience and existence. This includes recognizing the connection between all people, all things, and ultimately the connection between you and the divine, or you and God. To do this, according to transpersonal psychology, you must move beyond traditional conscious experiences and traditional ways of knowing. Transpersonal psychology respects many nontraditional means of gaining information, such as intuition, psychic phenomena, and spiritual, religious, or mystical experiences. Among the goals many transpersonal therapists share is the goal of helping you find the purpose of your life, as well as the purposes of events that appeared to happen to you accidentally.

The power of prayer. A 1999 study by John Maltby and colleagues in the *British Journal of Health Psychology* found that people who prayed frequently were also less likely to suffer from depression or anxiety. A 2006 report by Daniel Hall in the *Journal of the American Board of Family Medicine* also reported that people who went to church every week appeared to extend their lives by two to three years.

Another goal is to help you find a connection between your body, mind, and spirit. Many transpersonal psychologists believe that the psychological, spiritual, and emotional development of each person is part of the bigger evolution of the human species and the universe as a whole. According to influential transpersonal theorist Ken Wilber, spiritual development is the ultimate purpose of life and the true aim of transpersonal psychology.

As with other models of psychotherapy highlighted in this book, there isn't just one form of transpersonal psychology. Many transpersonal psychotherapists utilize meditation techniques and methods of prayer, but they may also use techniques from other types of psychotherapy.

Transpersonal psychology can be effective for:

- Self-growth and personal insight
- Spiritual development

For more information, visit the website of:

- The Association for Transpersonal Psychology: www.atpweb.org

Now you try it: *Describe your own "big-picture" philosophy or spiritual beliefs. How do they influence the way you live? Ideally, how would you like them to influence your life? Have you ever had a spiritual experience, even a small one? How did that affect your life?*

CHAPTER 4

Insight-Oriented Treatments

This chapter includes psychoanalysis and two treatments that are largely based on psychoanalysis. Psychoanalysis is the original form of psychotherapy that was created by the work of two Austrian physicians, Sigmund Freud and Josef Breuer. Around 1880, it was Breuer who successfully treated "Anna O." for her headaches and other physical symptoms by hypnotizing her and having her talk about emotionally charged events from her past. Breuer and his colleague, Freud, discussed Anna's case at length and believed that the "hysteria" from which she suffered (actually a conversion disorder) was caused by painful emotions that had been suppressed from her conscious awareness. They believed that by getting her to talk about those events, she was able to release the emotions and relieve her symptoms.

Soon, the two clinicians were treating other members of Viennese society for similar physical and emotional symptoms. However, the two disagreed over how the memories were suppressed in the first place, and they soon parted company. The break with Breuer would be the first of many broken professional relationships for Freud, including those with two other psychiatrists discussed in this chapter, Carl Jung and Alfred Adler. Shortly after, Freud also abandoned hypnosis but he continued to use and develop the "talking cure" that had been successful with Anna O. This would not be the last time that Freud would revise and improve his techniques.

Jung's analytical psychotherapy incorporates elements of psychoanalysis with spirituality, art, and a "library" of universal roles that we all live out. Adler's individual psychology focuses on your relationships and social responsibility. Freud's psychoanalysis, now also known as psychodynamic therapy, continues to focus on uncovering your unconscious thoughts and examining the relationship between you and your therapist.

As with the humanistic therapies, these psychoanalytic treatments are also hard to standardize, study, and compare to other treatments for problems such as anxiety and depression. As a result, you'll notice that the first two treatments are mainly recommended for self-growth and personal insight. This is not to imply that they are unimportant or ineffective treatments, but we do suggest that you first consider other treatments if you're struggling with a specific, identifiable problem, such as panic disorder.

ANALYTICAL PSYCHOTHERAPY/
JUNGIAN PSYCHOTHERAPY

Analytical psychotherapy, or *Jungian psychotherapy*, was developed by Carl Jung, a Swiss psychiatrist, at the turn of the twentieth century. Originally, Jung was a close friend of Sigmund Freud and a practitioner of Freud's psychoanalysis. However, after a series of disagreements, the two friends parted company and Jung went on to develop his own form of psychotherapy, which shares some of its basic theories and practices with psychoanalysis.

Like psychoanalysis, analytical psychotherapy uses the relationship between you and your therapist as a method of examining your relationship problems. Analytical psychotherapy also believes in conscious and unconscious thoughts that influence your health and behaviors. However, Jung also believed that your soul, or *psyche*, is just as important as unconscious and conscious thoughts, and that it's the awareness of all three elements that helps you make sense of your life and the world at large.

A unique principle of analytical psychotherapy is the belief in a *collective unconscious* that is shared by all of humanity. The collective unconscious is viewed much like a spiritual library that holds universal patterns of personality and ideas, a library from which you frequently receive knowledge without knowing that you're doing so. Jung studied art from many parts of the world and, through his studies, he recognized that very different cultures share similar symbols and myths, a similarity that he thought is caused by more than mere coincidence. Jung believed that what he called the collective unconscious greatly influences the lives of people across the boundaries of distance and time.

From the collective unconscious, humans often borrow universal personality patterns, called *archetypes*, which influence how we act and how we make choices. Among these patterns are popular roles that

---

A man of many interests. In addition to founding one of the earliest schools of psychotherapy, Carl Jung's other fields of study included mythology, spirituality, religion, Eastern philosophy, psychic phenomena, and UFOs.

---

we take on, roles that are often found in many cultures' mythologies and stories, such as the Hero, the Earth Mother, the Trickster, and the Outcast. These universal archetypes also include certain significant situations in life, such as the Quest, the Initiation, and the Journey. An analytical psychotherapist will often reframe your life using one of these archetypes. This is done to help you figure out the expectations and obstacles that you might be encountering and the various ways in which these obstacles might be overcome.

Analytical psychotherapy is also based on the principle of balancing opposites, such as illness and health. Jung believed that symptoms of illness also hold clues that will help you recover. For example, one of the ways this occurs is through an awareness of the *shadow*. The shadow is that part of yourself that you don't want to acknowledge or recognize. However, when you deny that your shadow-self exists, you push it further into the unconscious part of your mind, where, eventually, it finds a way of manifesting itself as a problem.

For example, if you don't want to admit that you're capable of cheating other people, you might be constantly afraid that other people are trying to cheat you. If you were seeing an analytical therapist, he or she might suggest that in order for this fear to subside, you must recognize your shadow, that is, your own capacity to cheat. This doesn't mean that you need to engage in cheating behaviors, but you do need to acknowledge that part of yourself is being suppressed and denied.

Clues about the shadow-self can often be found in your dreams, which are an important element of treatment in analytical psychotherapy. Dreams often contain hidden symbolism and archetypes that can help you solve your problems.

Analytical psychotherapy tries to help you find balance in other aspects of your life, too. This includes recognizing the male and female roles that we all take on, no matter what our gender. It also includes finding a balance in the way you interact with other people. Jung believed that we use four modes for taking in information: thinking, feeling, sensing, and being intuitive. He also believed that everyone is naturally inclined toward being introverted or extroverted. An analytical therapist will help you examine these aspects of your life and, ultimately, help you find a healthy balance between them.

In practice, analytical psychotherapy can be a very creative process. Some analytical therapists help their clients learn to use their imagination through writing, visualization, painting, and storytelling. Sometimes, this creative process also includes making elaborate scenes in sandboxes using different figures, symbols, and representations.

Finally, analytical psychotherapy also puts a great emphasis on helping you examine your future, not just your past. Jung recognized that it wasn't enough for some of his clients just to solve their immediate problems. Many of them wanted to continue forming a deeper understanding of themselves and their goals in life.

Analytical psychotherapy can be effective for:

- Self-growth and personal insight
- Spiritual development

For more information, visit the websites of:

- The C. G. Jung Institute of San Francisco: www.sfjung.org
- The International Association for Analytical Psychology: www.iaap.org

Now you try it: *Play. Be creative. Draw. Write a song. Play an instrument. Sing a song. Paint. Tell a story. Explore a part of your creativity that you've been ignoring or denying. Just do it and notice how it makes you feel.*

INDIVIDUAL PSYCHOLOGY

Individual psychology was created by Alfred Adler, an Austrian psychiatrist, at the beginning of the twentieth century. Originally, Adler was an early colleague of Sigmund Freud, who invited Adler in 1902 to join his circle of psychoanalysts at their Wednesday evening meetings in Vienna. Although Adler soon became president of the early psychoanalytic society, he and Freud quickly dissolved their personal and professional relationship in 1911, just as Freud and Jung would later do in 1914.

Unlike Freud, Adler believed that you can be understood only as a whole being, and not as separate, often opposing, forces. Your thoughts, feelings, behaviors, dreams, and physical-being all work together, moving you in the same direction. Similarly, Adler's theory is very much a psychology of social relatedness and connectedness, despite its name, "individual psychology," which in German refers to the indivisible, unique qualities of each person. Adler believed that you are an inseparable part of society at large: your family, country, universe, and so forth; and, so, you must find a healthy connection to that society to feel fulfilled.

Whether you feel connected or disconnected to others depends on your *style of life*. A person with a healthy style of life has learned how to contribute to his or her society and the welfare of others while simultaneously taking care of his or her own needs, especially work, community, and loving relationships. When a person with a healthy style of life encounters difficulties, he or she will use creative strategies to overcome those problems. In individual psychology, this is known as overcoming feelings of *inferiority*.

However, others are not as capable of balancing personal and social needs, often because they did not receive the necessary support in childhood to overcome obstacles and difficulties. As a result, these

If you can't beat 'em ... Adler himself struggled to overcome early feelings of inferiority. When he was five and suffering with an exceptionally serious case of pneumonia, his family's physician didn't think he'd live. Upon surviving, Adler strove for superiority by deciding to become a medical doctor himself.

people struggle with strong feelings of unworthiness, or they develop an *inferiority complex*, which often leads to an unhealthy or *mistaken style of life*. To compensate for their feelings of unworthiness, these people often engage in activities that make them feel superior to others. They pursue goals such as wealth, success, and power instead of finding healthier ways to cope with their problems.

When treating someone with an unhealthy style of life, a therapist using individual psychology will examine the ways in which the person's life is guided by a particular purpose or goal. In this way, individual psychology is future-oriented (as opposed to Freud's psychoanalysis, which focuses more on the past). A person with an unhealthy style of life might be moving toward a goal that is unconsciously chosen, realistic or unrealistic, or toward a goal in which the person is striving for superiority. Individual psychology is a collaborative process between you and the therapist that is often time-limited and focused on a specific problem. Ultimately, the aim is to uncover and explore your goals, to create a healthy style of life that balances both your personal needs and your social responsibility, and to correct *basic mistakes*, which are the dysfunctional thoughts and attitudes you have about yourself and others.

A therapist using individual psychology will often act as your "coach," giving you direction and inspiring confidence. The process also often involves the use of guided imagery, exploration of your early memories, role-playing, questionnaires, and other creative techniques that require you to play an active role in your treatment.

Individual psychology can be effective for:

- Self-growth and personal insight
- Treating problems relating to others

For more information, visit the websites of:

- The North American Society of Adlerian Psychology: www.alfredadler.org
- The Adlerian Society of the U.K.: www.adleriansociety.co.uk

Now you try it: *Contemplate the goal or goals that are influencing your life. Record some ideas about how those goals are influencing the decisions you make in your life. Are those decisions making your life more fulfilling or more distressing? If necessary, how might changing your goals affect the decisions you make, and therefore, how you live your life?*

PSYCHOANALYSIS/PSYCHODYNAMIC THERAPY

Psychoanalysis, largely developed by Sigmund Freud in the late nineteenth century, was the first form of psychotherapy. Freud based his treatment on what he found to be helpful for his clients, and like all good scientists, he consistently revised his theories when he was presented with new evidence that didn't fit with his older ideas. As a result, psychoanalysis is a treatment that has undergone much revision, by Freud and his later followers. It's also a theory that's been defined differently by the different mental health care professionals who practice it. As a result, there's no single explanation of what psychoanalytic treatment is.

Mental health care professionals who use this form of treatment are called *psychoanalysts*. Some of them have abandoned a number of Freud's earlier ideas, such as the *Oedipus complex* (the belief that a child sexually desires his or her opposite-sex parent), while other professionals have retained some of those earlier ideas. Today it's common for many mental health professionals to refer to the treatment they use as "psychodynamic therapy," to differentiate themselves from some of the earlier forms of psychoanalysis. But, for our purposes here, it's probably good enough for you to know some of the basic principles on which both treatments are based, which we'll just refer to as "psychoanalysis."

One widely held principle emphasizes the key role of the unconscious mind. According to psychoanalysis, our thoughts, beliefs, and awareness work in a multilayered way. (Imagine an iceberg floating in the ocean; you can see only the tip above the surface, but below the surface lies a much more massive chunk of ice.) Some thoughts are fully within your awareness and are called *conscious thoughts* (the tip of the iceberg). Some thoughts are almost within your awareness and are called *preconscious thoughts* (the ice just below the surface). And some thoughts are beyond your awareness, these are called your *unconscious thoughts* (the majority of the iceberg that lies deep beneath the surface). One of the goals of psychoanalysis is to bring the deeper, unconscious, hidden thoughts to the surface of your conscious awareness.

Some psychoanalysts also believe that the mind is organized according to the roles it plays in helping you solve problems. This is famously known as the id, ego, and superego division. The *id* represents your instinctual, childlike needs and impulses. The *superego* is often thought of as the parental rule-maker, since it imposes morality and standards. And the *ego* is left to make decisions based on the needs of both the id and the superego, while also dealing with the requirements of your everyday reality.

According to one of Freud's later theories, a person becomes anxious when an unpleasant thought attempts to "bubble up" from the unconsciousness level to the conscious level of awareness. At this point, the ego uses a series of *defense mechanisms* to keep those kinds of thoughts hidden, and thus "helps" you avoid feeling scared or nervous.

Here are some (poorly) described examples of defense mechanisms. However, keep in mind that, in reality, you're usually not aware that you're using defense mechanisms:

- **Displacement:** Shifting the target of your anger or other feelings from the original source to someone or something less threatening. ("I'm not mad because my boss just fired me after twenty years of dedicated service. I'm mad because you always greet me at the door in that same stupid way: 'Hi honey. How was work today?' What kind of crap is that?")

- **Rationalization:** Justifying your feelings or behaviors in order to avoid feeling guilty. ("Sure I stole the money

from the bank, but don't blame me. If you really wanted
your money to be safe, you should have buried it in your
backyard.")

■ **Projection:** Accusing someone else of thinking or acting
in an unpleasant way, when it's really you who thinks or
acts this way. ("I'm not the one getting angry! You're the
one getting angry! I'm just screaming at the top of my
lungs because I want to make sure you hear me!")

■ **Reaction formation:** Acting in the opposite way of how
you really feel. ("Sure, you just destroyed my priceless
collection of *Superman* comics, Bill. But come here and
let me give you a hug anyway.")

■ **Regression:** Reverting to an earlier, immature manner
of behavior. ("If you don't stop yelling at me, I'll just sit in
the corner with my bottle and blanket and cry.")

■ **Intellectualization:** Denying or avoiding how you feel
with excessive thinking. ("Yes, emotion—or affect as it's
also known, is a very primitive form of communication
that begins in the limbic system of the brain and travels to
the body via the autonomic nervous system. Luckily, I'm
never bothered by it.")

■ **Sublimation:** Channeling your anger or other unpleasant emotions into healthier, more socially acceptable
activities. ("Instead of hitting you over the head, like
I want to, I'm going to paint a picture of me hitting you
over the head.")

■ **Undoing:** Performing a repetitive ritual in order to avoid some feeling. ("Danger? What danger? I'm just washing the dishes, over and over and over again. No big deal. I just want to make sure they're really, really clean.")

■ **Repression:** An unpleasant thought gets "locked" in your unconscious level of awareness and is prevented from rising to the conscious level. ("Repression? No, I can't remember repressing a single thought in my entire life.")

Another principle of psychoanalytic treatment states that the origin of mental health problems often lies in childhood. According to psychoanalysis, children pass through unique developmental phases that are related to biological functions such as breast-feeding and toilet training. It's believed that if you experience difficulties during one of these phases, and have problems getting your needs met, you'll later develop problems related to that phase. Equally as damaging can be the way that you were treated (or mistreated) in your childhood by a parent, family member, or other person.

Many psychoanalysts believe in the influence of unconscious drives or instincts that also guide your life. One of the most common is the drive to seek pleasure, called the *libido*. Other psychoanalysts

Keeping it in the family. One of Sigmund Freud's most interesting cases was the psychoanalysis he conducted on his twenty-three-year-old daughter, Anna, who would later go on to become a famous psychoanalyst herself by extending her father's work to the treatment of children and further writing about the role of the ego and defense mechanisms.

> *Most psychoanalysts will allow you to talk in a very free and unguided way. This is called* free association.

believe that all of your thoughts, feelings, and actions are determined by your past experiences. According to this belief, nothing happens by accident, and if you look hard enough, with the help of a psychoanalyst, you can figure out what happened in your past that caused you to act the way you do in the present.

Psychoanalysts also use specific treatment methods in session. Some clients are surprised when they enter psychoanalysis because their therapist is very quiet and doesn't say much or offer any advice on how to fix their problems. Instead, most psychoanalysts will allow you to talk in a very free and unguided way. This is called *free association*. Later, when the analyst has heard enough information to make an informed observation, he or she will then interpret what is happening in your life. By doing this, the analyst is trying to help you become aware of your unconscious thoughts and the defenses you're using, to help you resolve and work through your unconscious conflicts.

It's also common for psychoanalysts to talk about the relationship you have with them, to examine the problems you may have in your other personal relationships. For example, it's believed that a client will often treat the analyst in the same way that the client treated a parent. This is called *transference*. When this occurs, your analyst will inform you to help you resolve the unsettled conflict that you might have had with your parent.

Many psychoanalysts will also frequently ask their clients to discuss their dreams. Early in his career, Freud stated that the best way to discover anyone's unconscious thoughts and, possibly, the origin of the client's problem is to investigate the person's dreams, because that is where Freud believed unconscious desires are most freely expressed.

In addition to psychoanalysis and psychodynamic therapy, many related treatments share similar principles but focus on different elements. For example, *object relations therapy* emphasizes the different relationships a person has and how those relationships are thought about and dealt with, while *control-mastery therapy* believes that people want to solve their problems and have unconscious plans to do so that must be discovered. (And no, it doesn't involve leather and whips.)

Psychoanalysis is effective for treating:

- Antisocial personality disorder
- Bipolar disorder-related issues
- Dependent personality disorder
- Dissociative disorders
- Borderline personality disorder
- Paranoid personality disorder
- Schizoid personality disorder
- Self-growth and personal insight
- Narcissistic personality disorder

For more information, visit the websites of:

- The American Psychoanalytic Association: www.apsa.org

- The National Association for the Advancement of Psychoanalysis: www.naap.org

- San Francisco Control Mastery Research Group: www.sfprg.org

Now you try it: *Lie down on a sofa or a bed in a quiet room where you won't be disturbed. Pick a topic from your life and just start talking about it out loud. Say whatever comes to mind, even if it seems unrelated or disturbing. Just keep following your trail of thoughts out loud, without censoring what you say or think. Observe where your thoughts take you. Record the session if you want, and listen to it later to determine if your free association brought you to a different understanding of the topic than you started with.*

CHAPTER 5

Unconventional (But Effective) Treatments

The following treatments aren't easy to categorize because they use nontraditional techniques. By that, we mean these treatments aren't often taught in graduate or medical school programs. However, four of them are well supported by research: biofeedback, electroconvulsive therapy, hypnosis, and light therapy. And the other two are based on techniques that are almost as old as modern, human civilization: mindfulness therapy and somatic therapy. Chances are that you won't just stumble upon these treatments unless you go looking for them. They will probably be harder to find because they require either special equipment or specially trained clinicians. However, for some problems, it will definitely be worth your efforts to find these treatments.

In this chapter, you'll read about six of these unconventional treatments. Biofeedback uses tools to help you monitor, measure, and control your body's physical responses to stress and other stimuli. Electroconvulsive therapy, also known as electroshock therapy, uses electricity to treat people struggling with severe depression and other symptoms. Hypnosis, although it's gotten a bad rap from old movies and stage performers, is actually very effective for treating many problems. Light therapy uses sunlight to beat the winter blues. Mindfulness therapy uses meditation and other techniques to help you refocus on your health. And somatic therapies incorporate talking with healing forms of touch and massage.

BIOFEEDBACK

Biofeedback is a treatment that mainly began in the 1960s. It often uses electronic equipment to help you monitor some of your body's responses to your thoughts, feelings, and other stimuli. By monitoring those responses the goal is to help you learn to control and change your body's responses and, at the same time, also change the way you feel emotionally and physically.

As an example, you can think of a simple thermometer as a form of biofeedback. When you're not feeling well, you take your temperature with the thermometer to see if your body temperature is high or low. Then, as you take steps to make yourself feel better, you continue to use the thermometer to determine if your efforts are successful. Similarly, you might use a bathroom scale to monitor your efforts to gain or lose weight. Both instruments are forms of biofeedback; they literally give you feedback about your body's physical responses. And, as in all forms of biofeedback, the equipment itself doesn't make the changes for you, but merely gives you information; it is always you who makes the changes.

Biofeedback can be used as a treatment for many problems but, often, it's used to help a person learn to relax. This is often accomplished by using biofeedback that measures the person's skin temperature, heart rate, muscle tension, sweat output on the skin, breathing rate, or brain wave pattern. When you are anxious, nervous, scared, or frightened, your body experiences a predictable pattern of changes: your hands and feet get cold and clammy, your heart rate speeds up, muscle tension increases, breathing rate increases, and brain wave activity becomes more erratic. These are all results of the *sympathetic nervous system* response, also called the *fight, flight, or freeze system*.

This system prepares you for three possible responses: to run away from a dangerous situation, to stay and confront the danger, or to stay still and possibly avoid the situation. This nervous system response is a survival mechanism that happens automatically, without you having to think about it. For example, if you were crossing the street and saw a strange-looking person coming at you from out of the shadows, chances are that your sympathetic nervous system response would automatically be triggered to help you survive. Either you would run away or you would prepare to confront the person (hopefully, you wouldn't freeze, as possums are apt to do).

Not all situations are as life-threatening as this, yet your body often responds in this same way. Sometimes, just thinking about the daily stressors of life, worrying about the future, or remembering past events is enough to trigger the sympathetic response. Then, not only are you thinking anxious thoughts, but you also start to feel anxious as your heart rate, muscle tension, sweat output, breathing, and temperature all become affected. Here is where biofeedback can be most effective, when it helps you monitor those sympathetic responses and gain more control over them.

For example, suppose a woman sought help for anxiety by using biofeedback. Using a small temperature sensor from the monitor attached to her finger, she might be told to imagine some of her anxious thoughts. It's likely she would see a drop in her temperature on the biofeedback monitor. Then, after being taught relaxation and visualization techniques, such as imagining her hands getting heavy and warm, she might learn to make the temperature in her finger rise. This would interrupt the sympathetic nervous system response and, therefore, also

The truth, the whole truth, and ... The polygraph, or "lie detector test," uses biofeedback equipment to measure a person's responses to anxiety-provoking questions. Unfortunately, however, not everyone's nervous system responds the same way to lying, and some people can fake their way through the test.

lead to a simultaneous sensation of calmness.

> *Biofeedback is generally best for people who want to be active in their healing process.*

Or suppose that a man sought help for a burning pain in his forearm. He would probably be monitored with muscle biofeedback equipment that measures the small electrical charges made during muscle activity. Again, using relaxation and imagery techniques, perhaps focusing on the specific muscles becoming looser and more relaxed, the man would learn to control the muscle tension.

But, remember, the biofeedback equipment doesn't make the changes for you; you are always in control of all your responses. As such, biofeedback is generally best for people who want to be active in their healing process, for people who are prepared to practice techniques such as relaxation, and for people who have a history of patiently practicing other skills, such as sports, music, art, and so forth.

Biofeedback is effective for treating:

- Anxiety
- Attention-deficit/ hyperactivity disorder (ADHD)
- Breathing problems
- Chronic physical pain issues
- Constipation and incontinence
- Conversion disorder

- Headaches
- Hypertension
- Insomnia
- Irritable bowel syndrome
- Phobias
- Raynaud's syndrome
- Stress
- Substance abuse-related issues

For more information, visit the websites of:

- The Association of Applied Psychophysiology and
  Biofeedback: www.aapb.org

- The Biofeedback Certification Institute of America:
  bcia.affiniscape.com

Now you try it: *Get a basic weather thermometer, the kind you hang outside to measure air temperature. Hold the bulb of the thermometer between your thumb and forefinger for about ten seconds. Write down your starting temperature. It's probably between 75 and 95 degrees Fahrenheit (23 and 35 degrees Celsius). Now, while still holding the thermometer, think of something peaceful, relaxing, or soothing for two to three minutes. Maybe imagine yourself on your ideal vacation. Did your temperature rise? It should. Practice this often and try to make your temperature rise above 90 degrees Fahrenheit (32 degrees Celsius).*

ELECTROCONVULSIVE THERAPY

Electroconvulsive therapy (ECT), once called "electroshock therapy," is not a form of talk therapy, but it is a treatment that's sometimes used to treat severe mental health problems such as depression, psychosis, and mania; so, it's worth mentioning. Usually, ECT is the last alternative for treating a severe depression that's often accompanied by delusions or suicidal thoughts, especially when the depression hasn't responded to other forms of treatment, such as medications or psychotherapy. ECT is a hospital procedure in which patients are first given a muscle relaxant and anesthesia to sedate them. Then an electric current is sent through one or both sides of their brain for about half a second. This causes seizures, or convulsions, in the brain for about fifteen seconds, which eventually lead to a lessening of depressive or psychotic symptoms. This treatment is usually conducted six to twelve times and is spread out over the course of two to four weeks.

Despite improvements to this technique since it was first introduced in the 1940s, often ECT still leads to temporary problems with remembering new information, which can last several months; some permanent loss of older memories; and some general confusion in the hours following the treatment. Yet, despite these issues, many patients have found lasting relief from their depression using ECT when all other methods have failed.

Shocking, but true. Dick Cavett (talk-show host) and Kitty Dukakis (wife of a former Massachusetts governor) both credit ECT for successfully treating their depression. Dukakis has even written a book about it called *Shock: The Healing Power of Electroconvulsive Therapy.*

Electroconvulsive therapy is effective for treating:

- Severe cases of depression, mania, and psychosis that have not responded to other forms of treatment

For more information, visit the website of:

- The American Psychiatric Association: www.psych.org/research/apire/training_fund/clin_res/index.cfm

Now you try it: *Get a diesel-powered generator and a pair of jumper cables... We're only kidding.* Do not attempt to shock yourself with electricity in any way imaginable. This is extremely dangerous and potentially lethal. *Leave this treatment to the professionals.*

HYPNOTHERAPY

Hypnosis has been used to treat mental health problems for over two hundred years. Its utilization began in late eighteenth-century France, where patients were mesmerized and relieved of their symptoms using magnets and the power of suggestion. Later, in the 1840s, James Braid, a Scottish medical doctor, used the technique as an anesthesia for his patients, but he realized that the magnets were unnecessary for the method to work. He then renamed the treatment hypnosis, from the Greek word "hypnos," meaning "sleep." The technique was even used by Sigmund Freud to treat patients, before he created psychoanalysis.

Unfortunately, hypnosis has suffered much at the hands of the popular media. Today, it's largely thought of only for its entertainment value. However, *hypnotherapy*—the psychotherapeutic form of hypnosis—is officially recognized by both the American Psychological Association and the American Medical Association as an effective treatment for certain conditions. It's been shown to be effective for reducing symptoms of chronic pain, relieving symptoms of phobias, improving sports performance, easing childbirth, and in some cases helping to stop cigarette smoking. Many other uses for hypnotherapy have also been successfully applied, and research has shown that hypnosis has a direct, observable effect on the brain.

Many people expect to be put into a sleeplike trance when they undergo hypnotherapy. However, this is another misconception. *Hypnosis* is a state of deep relaxation in which you become more receptive to suggestions made by your hypnotherapist. Unlike in the movies, your hypnotherapist will probably not use a swinging pendulum to induce your hypnotic state. Instead, you will most likely be asked to concentrate on the sound of your hypnotherapist's voice as he or she guides you into a state of deep relaxation. This can be done with guided visualization, in which you imagine a peaceful scene, or you might be

> **Don't believe everything you think.** Despite popular claims in the media, hypnosis is not an effective tool for recovering lost memories. In fact, some research suggests that hypnosis can create very believable but very false memories.

asked to imagine different parts of your body becoming heavy and tired.

After leading you through a few sessions of hypnosis, your hypnotherapist might ask you to try self-hypnotic techniques on your own, perhaps with the use of a recorded session. This additional work can strengthen the effects of your hypnotherapy.

Despite the benefits of hypnotherapy, it should be noted that not everyone will be helped by the treatment. People who believe that hypnotism might work on them tend to be the ones for whom it's more effective. But, according to research and estimates, 10 percent of the general population can't be easily hypnotized.

Hypnosis is often effective for treating:

- Depression
- Dissociative identity disorder (multiple personalities)
- Eating disorders (anorexia and bulimia)
- Obesity
- Pain (acute and chronic)
- Performance anxiety
- Phobias
- Post-traumatic stress disorder
- Smoking habits

For more information, visit the websites of:

- The American Hypnosis Association:
  www.hypnosis.edu/aha/

- The American Association of Professional Hypnotherapists:
  www.aaph.org

- The American Psychological Association Society of
  Psychological Hypnosis: www.apa.org/divisions/div30/

Now you try it: Autogenics *is a relaxing form of self-hypnosis. Find an undisturbed, comfortable place to sit with your eyes closed. Silently say to yourself, "My arms are heavy" three times, and each time, scan your arms for any feelings of heaviness. Then say to yourself, "My arms are warm" three times and, again, scan your arms for any feelings of warmth. After you notice the desired effects, try these phrases: "My heartbeat is calm and regular." "My breathing is smooth and even," and "My stomach is comfortably warm." Then at the end of each complete session, say "And I am at peace," and notice any soothing sensations.*

LIGHT THERAPY/PHOTOTHERAPY

Light therapy, also called *phototherapy,* is an effective treatment for *seasonal affective disorder* (SAD), a form of depression caused by deficient exposure to sunlight. Many people suffer with SAD during the fall and winter months, and in countries closer to the north and south poles, when the number of daylight hours sharply declines. Many people struggling with SAD recognize that the symptoms of their depression begin at approximately the same time each year and then lift during the spring, when the sunlight returns. Simply put, light therapy involves regular exposure to special lighting devices that emit a bright light that simulates sunlight. (Another alternative includes taking a sunny winter vacation every year.)

Exposure to sunlight is important to healthy living for a number of reasons. First, it controls the human body's twenty-four-hour sleep-wake cycle, also known as the *circadian rhythm.* Exposure to bright light signals the body that it's time to be active (which is why you should avoid bright lights like television screens and computer monitors if you're having trouble falling asleep at night).

Second, when the sunlight disappears during the hours of darkness, the pineal gland in the brain releases *melatonin,* which makes you feel tired and sluggish, preparing you to fall asleep. This normal process becomes a problem for people with SAD during the darker months of fall and winter because the pineal gland releases excess melatonin, causing the person to feel tired and sluggish during waking hours and disturbing his or her sleep at night. By using light therapy for several

---

You can't fool Mother Nature. Melatonin, the hormone that controls the human sleep-wake cycle, also controls winter hibernation in many other animals, like bears and ground squirrels.

---

hours a day, many people with SAD have found that their depression is greatly reduced or eliminated.

Light therapy is effective for treating:

- Seasonal affective disorder (SAD)

For more information, visit the website of:

- The American Psychological Association: www.apa.org/monitor/feb06/sad.html

Now you try it: *If you haven't had much time in the sunshine lately, go to a place that's sunny and bask in the sun's rays ... after applying your sunblock, of course. Notice any changes in the way you feel. And if the place where you live just isn't very sunny, consider taking a trip, even just a daylong trip, to someplace that is.*

MINDFULNESS THERAPY

Mindfulness therapy uses meditation and other techniques to help you focus your attention and build greater self-acceptance. This type of treatment borrows much of its philosophy and methods from Buddhist traditions, which use meditative practices to cultivate awareness, insight, and freedom from suffering. From a Western perspective, mindfulness techniques can also help you let go of thoughts and feelings that cause pain.

Meditation helps focus your attention on what you're experiencing and thinking in the present moment. By doing that, it also helps you become more aware of your immediate thoughts, feelings, and actions. This type of concentration takes practice, but it can have many benefits. Focusing on the present moment allows you to disengage from repetitious and painful thoughts about the past and future. It also gives you space to step back from your experience and understand what's really happening in a clearer way. This insight can then help you make a choice about how to act in the immediate moment instead of relying on automatic, habitual reactions.

There are two popular forms of mindfulness therapy. The first is *mindfulness-based stress reduction*, developed by biologist Jon Kabat-Zinn. This treatment was originally designed to help hospital patients reduce their levels of stress and pain by using meditation techniques and yoga. It's usually taught in an eight-to-ten-week course, but you'll also be expected to practice the techniques on a daily basis at home, by yourself. The techniques used in this treatment focus on your breathing and the

> *Focusing on the present moment allows you to disengage from repetitious and painful thoughts about the past and future.*

Therapy or religion? Although the techniques most often used in mindfulness therapy are Buddhist in nature, like meditation, the truth is, nearly every major religion uses some form of mindfulness practice, such as prayer, contemplation, chanting, ritual, and song.

---

feelings in your body. When distractions arise, you'll be instructed to notice them without getting hooked into them or forming any opinions about them. You'll also be instructed not to judge yourself for becoming distracted.

A similar treatment is called *mindfulness-based cognitive therapy*, which also incorporates elements of cognitive behavioral therapy to help you observe your experiences, thoughts, and emotions. Yet again, one of the key goals is to help you observe your experiences without making judgments about them.

Of the many possible results, mindfulness techniques like these often lead to a greater tolerance of distressing situations, greater relaxation, a change in thinking styles, the development of less judgmental views of yourself and your experiences, and an increase in skills for coping with difficult situations. In studies, mindfulness therapy has resulted in positive effects on the immune system; reduced chronic pain; decreased binge eating; lessened stress in cancer patients; decreased repetitive, sad thinking in depressed patients; and reduced odds of having another major depressive episode.

Mindfulness therapy is effective for treating:

- Anger-control problems

- General stress

- Pain disorders

For more information, visit the website of:

• The Center for Mindfulness: www.umassmed.edu/cfm/

Now you try it: *Find a comfortable place to sit where you'll be undisturbed for ten minutes. Close your eyes and place one hand over your belly button. Find a slow, natural rhythm of breathing that takes in neither too much nor too little air. Slowly inhale through your nose and imagine your breath moving down into your belly, making it expand like a balloon. Then, slowly exhale through your mouth, like you're blowing out candles, and feel your belly deflate. When you become distracted by your thoughts—and you will—gently return your focus to your breathing. Focus on breathing slowly and evenly like this for five to ten minutes, using a timer if necessary, and notice any feelings of relaxation.*

SOMATIC THERAPIES

Somatic therapies are a category of treatments that emphasize the connection between your body, thoughts, and emotions. *Soma* means "body" in Greek, and often these types of treatments focus on healing the body in order to provide relief from physical, mental, and emotional pain. These treatments are also referred to as *body-oriented therapies.*

Many of these treatments share the principle that emotions can be stored in the body, and hidden emotions can be experienced and released through body movements and adjustments. This is often accomplished through techniques like massage or deep tissue manipulations, such as *Rolfing.* However, many forms of somatic therapy combine these or similar techniques with general principles of psychotherapy. Often, somatic therapy will include general massage, light physical touch, deep tissue manipulation, relaxation techniques, movement, or exercise.

Like many types of somatic therapies, the *Rosen Method* uses gentle touch to release muscle tension. According to this theory, this process often causes old memories and feelings to reemerge. It's often used to treat pain and frequently used in conjunction with many of the other forms of therapy discussed in this book. *Hakomi experiential psychotherapy* uses mindfulness techniques to focus your attention on your physical habits and expressions, and then explores painful memories that are often attached to them.

Process-oriented psychology is based on many principles from Jungian analytical therapy. In addition to focusing on the connection between your mind and body, it also examines your dreams and how they influence your life.

> **Soma *means "body" in Greek, and often these types of treatments focus on healing the body in order to provide relief from physical, mental, and emotional pain.***

117

The original form of therapy? Ayurvedic medicine is a theory of health care that originated in India over five thousand years ago. Among its many techniques, it uses massage, meditation, yoga, and herbal remedies.

Somatic therapies can be effective for:

- Treating body aches and pains
- Self-growth and personal insight

For more information, visit the websites of:

- The American Massage Therapy Association: www.amtamassage.org
- The Rolf Institute: www.rolf.org
- The Rosen Institute: www.rosenmethod.org
- The Hakomi Institute: www.hakomiinstitute.com
- The Process Work Institute: www.processwork.org

Now you try it: *Find a friend, spouse, or partner who is willing to exchange five minutes of shoulder rubbing or foot massaging. Or, if you can afford one, go get a professional full-body massage. Then, sit back—or lie down—and relax.*

CHAPTER 6

Treatments for More Than One Person at a Time

Often, your problems will affect not only you, but also the people around you. In these cases, it might be beneficial for all of you to engage in therapy together, as a couple, a family, or as friends. This can be an effective way of treating both the problem that brought you all into therapy in the first place, and the other related effects that the problem has had on your lives. For example, we've often worked with families in which one parent has a drug or alcohol problem. But in addition to that big, identifiable problem, which often brings the family in for treatment, there are usually other issues that are just as important, such as communication difficulties between family members and feelings of resentment, anxiety, and anger. These other issues often serve to keep the more noticeable issue "alive," and unless they're addressed too, the bigger issue might never be solved.

In this chapter, you'll learn about three different treatments designed to help multiple people. Couples therapy focuses on treating problems that are affecting the lives of two people in some kind of relationship. Emotionally focused therapy is a newer, brief form of treatment that examines basic, underlying emotions and the human need for attachment. And, finally, family therapy is a group of treatments that focuses on how a presenting problem is affecting the lives of everyone involved.

COUPLES THERAPY

Naturally, *couples therapy* focuses on helping people who are involved in some kind of relationship. This usually means two people, but it can certainly include more, and it usually involves people in some kind of romantic relationship (such as married couples, partnerships, boyfriends, or girlfriends), but recently, we've heard of brothers, roommates, and even business partners who have all entered couples therapy to resolve their differences. Traditionally, this type of treatment has also been referred to as "marital therapy," but due to the modern abundance of nonmarried couples who often seek help, "couples therapy" is a more accurate description.

As anyone who's been in couples therapy will tell you, it can be a complicated process because there are always at least three "living beings" involved (which doesn't even include your therapist). You and your spouse or partner are the first two beings, and the relationship itself can be considered the third "being" whose survival depends on the others. As a result, couples therapy involves solving a combination of both individual and group problems.

Like some of the other therapies discussed in this book, couples therapy isn't one specific type of treatment. Many types of couples therapy use treatment models based on other therapies described in this book (like cognitive behavioral therapy or psychodynamic therapy). But as a category of related treatments, couples therapy focuses on many of the same issues.

Cognitive behavioral couples therapy looks at the way your actions and thoughts affect your partner's actions and thoughts and vice versa. At the heart of this treatment is the same theory as individual cognitive behavioral therapy: that is, behaviors that are rewarded tend to be repeated, and behavior that's punished won't be repeated. As a result, your cognitive behavioral couples therapist will help you examine how you and your spouse or partner reinforce and shape each other's behaviors, for better or for worse. Not surprisingly, it's been observed that couples with fewer problems treat their partners in a more positive way. In comparison, couples with more problems have greater communication difficulties and communicate in more hostile ways.

Variations of this treatment, such as *behavioral marital therapy* focus more on creating behavioral changes rather than changing patterns of thoughts. *Integrative behavioral couples therapy* helps you and your partner understand why you both act the way you do and, with that understanding, helps you build deeper compassion and acceptance of each other.

A cognitive behavioral couples therapist will often help you and your spouse or partner explore new ways to handle distressing emotions, like anger and pain, which can interfere with effective communication and problem solving. Often it's observed that couples with problems don't pay full attention to each other and make pessimistic predictions about their relationships. In couples therapy, you might be invited to participate in role-playing scenarios, to figure out new ways of communicating, listening, and solving problems. Another common intervention is to initiate special days on which you and your partner make extra efforts to increase positive communications and perform actions that are normally overlooked in your daily life.

Relationships of the rich and famous. An August 2007 story in *Us* magazine quoted several celebrity couples who have turned to therapy for help with their relationships. Among them, actress Michelle Pfeiffer was quoted as saying that she and her husband, David E. Kelley, go to therapy because "we all have our baggage, and David and I are no different." Actor Patrick Dempsey said he and his wife, Jillian, see their therapist for regular relationship "checkups."

Psychoanalytic or *psychodynamic couples therapy* explores the previous relationships both you and your partner have had and assesses how they might be influencing your current relationship. According to this theory, the way you learn to relate to other people in your earlier relationships—especially your parents—serves as a model for how you will relate to other people when you're an adult. Many of these patterns, according to psychoanalysis, are unconscious. Therefore, part of the treatment involves helping you and your spouse or partner to become aware of your patterns. These insights can then help the two of you to make conscious adjustments to your relationship.

Systems theory explores the way you and your spouse or partner, and possibly your whole family, form a structured unit in which the actions of one member affect all of the other members. In systems theory, problems are addressed as cyclical patterns of behavior. One of the commonly held beliefs in systems theory is that the partnership, or family system, generally wants to remain the same, that is, unchanged, even if the relationships are problematic. This is called *homeostasis*.

One intervention that is often used in systems theory is reframing. *Reframing* redefines a problem in a new way, which can lead to better understanding and greater odds for successful change. For example, maybe you hold back all of your feelings in your relationship, which then causes your partner to spend more time with friends. In such a case, your therapist might help both of you understand the cyclical nature of this problem, create a new framework for conceptualizing it, and then help you work toward making positive changes in a new way.

These are just a few examples of different types of couples therapies. It's probably possible to find a couples therapist who practices from any one of the modalities described in this book. In addition, many couples therapists also use techniques described later in the "family therapy" description, as the two techniques are often related.

Couples therapy is effective for treating:

- Alcohol and drug problems of a spouse or partner
- Bipolar disorder-related issues of a spouse or partner
- Couples and relationship problems
- Dependent personality disorder of a spouse or partner
- Depression-related issues of a spouse or partner

For more information, visit the website of:

- The American Association for Marriage and Family Therapy: www.aamft.org

Now you try it: *Schedule some uninterrupted time to sit down and talk with your spouse, partner, boyfriend, or girlfriend about any troubling relationship issues that need to be resolved. Use "I" statements—as in "When that happens, I feel sad"—rather than "you" statements—as in "You're such a jerk for making me feel so sad." Talk about how the issues are making you feel without blaming the other person for what's going on. Who knows? With a little honesty and empathy, you might be able to resolve your issues without a therapist's help.*

EMOTIONALLY FOCUSED THERAPY

Emotionally focused therapy is a form of couples therapy developed in the 1980s by psychologists Sue Johnson and Les Greenberg. It is a brief treatment, often lasting from eight to twenty sessions, and since its creation, multiple studies have verified its effectiveness.

At the heart of emotionally focused therapy is *attachment theory*, which states that everyone has an instinctive need for healthy, loving relationships. In childhood, this need can be successfully fulfilled through a healthy attachment to a parent figure. In adulthood, however, it's often achieved through a healthy attachment to a partner or spouse. In satisfying adult relationships, there is regular, open communication between the partners about their feelings and needs, which results in each partner feeling safe, secure, and comforted.

However, in troubled relationships, one or both partners may feel that the stability of the relationship is threatened and, as a result, effective communication often stops. For example, if someone feels insecure about his or her relationship, or feels threatened by the idea that the relationship might end, that person might not express the way he or she truly feels, such as hurt, angry, or scared. Instead, he or she might act out in ways that are critical, defensive, or withdrawing. Then, in response, the other partner might act in similar ways, which would tend to damage the relationship even further.

Ending this cyclical pattern is one of the main goals of emotionally focused therapy, which involves specific interventions and three stages of treatment. In the first stage you'll learn to identify the repetitive cycle

> *In satisfying adult relationships, there is regular, open communication between the partners about their feelings and needs, which results in each partner feeling safe, secure, and comforted.*

125

> **Getting down to basics.** According to psychologists like Paul Ekman, certain "basic" emotions are expressed in the same way by people living in different cultures around the world. When subjects from different cultures are shown photographs of people who are feeling afraid, angry, disgusted, sad, happy, or surprised, the subjects are able to recognize the emotion displayed in the person's facial expression, even if the person in the photograph is from a different culture.

of problematic behaviors and reactions that exist in your relationship, as well as identify the underlying emotions that remain unexpressed or that are expressed in problematic ways. Emotionally focused therapy often focuses on helping you uncover your "basic" human emotions, such as anger, fear, happiness, sadness, hurt, shame, and surprise.

In the second stage, you and your spouse or partner will begin to identify what you need from your relationship and start integrating those needs into the relationship. For example, if one of your needs is to get more recognition for what you contribute to the relationship, your therapist will demonstrate new ways for the two of you to interact with each other in order to get those needs met in a respectful way.

Finally, in the third stage of treatment, you and your partner will continue to solve long-standing problems in the relationship using your new emotional awareness and communication skills.

Overall, your emotionally focused therapist will help you redefine the "dance" of your relationship. Your therapist will assist both of you in clarifying how you're truly feeling in the relationship, improve the way you communicate and interact with each other, and help you both reestablish a safe, secure emotional bond with one another.

Emotionally focused therapy is effective for treating:

- Couples and relationship problems
- Depression-related issues of a family member or partner
- Family problems
- Trauma-related issues of a family member or partner

For more information visit the website of:

- The Center for Emotionally Focused Therapy: www.eft.ca

Now you try it: *Keep an emotional journal for a week. Keep track of when you feel one of the basic human emotions throughout the day (anger, fear, happiness, sadness, hurt, shame, and surprise). Then note how you express those emotions and how your expressions affect your relationships. Remember, it's natural—and human—to feel these emotions, but some emotions, like happiness, are sometimes easier to express than others, like anger.*

FAMILY THERAPY

As the name implies, *family therapy* focuses on the relationships and interactions between family members. This treatment is often used to address problems between family members, couples, spouses, and partners. But family therapy is also very helpful when an identified problem appears to exist with a single member of a family, such as a depressed parent or an anxious child. Yet, even in a situation where the problem appears to be with one person, your family therapist will address that problem as a symptom of a nonfunctional family system.

Like many of the other therapies discussed in this book, family therapy isn't a single type of treatment. Instead, it's a category of related therapies that focus on many of the same principles. In general, they all focus on the family as an arrangement of interdependent people whose actions affect each other. In many of these therapies, the family is regarded as a system that's out of balance and resistant to change.

Problems often arise when family members use habitual modes of communication that don't work. Yet, even when this is true, the goal isn't to figure out which person is at fault; the goal is to figure out how to interrupt that cycle and solve the identified problems more effectively.

Your family therapist will want to explore the different kinds of interactions that take place between the members of your family, including how the members communicate with each other and how problems are addressed during times of conflict. Your psychotherapist will also want to explore the roles that each member fills in your family system. Sometimes the role a person takes on isn't the role that is usually expected, such as a young child taking care of the parent. Often, a role reversal like this is enough to cause many problems. Gender and cultural roles that members take on are also important and need to be explored, in order to identify their potential impact on the problem that brought the family into treatment.

128

A presidential first. Bill Clinton was the first U.S. president to admit that he'd been in therapy. While governor of Arkansas, Clinton, his mother, and his brother attended family therapy after his brother was arrested on cocaine charges. A few years later, Clinton admitted that he had to return to family therapy with his wife, this time following his affair with White House intern Monica Lewinsky.

One of the common models used in family therapy is called *structural family therapy*, developed by psychiatrist Salvador Minuchin, and as its name implies, it largely focuses on the way your family is structured. Using this approach, your psychotherapist will want to examine who makes the decisions for your family, who appears to be running the family, the different alliances that are formed within the family (for better or worse), and the boundaries that exist or don't between family members and people outside your family. Family members who are too involved with each other are said to be *enmeshed*, whereas members who don't interact are *disengaged*. Using structural family therapy, a therapist will try to blend in with your family during sessions in order to better understand how your family operates, and eventually, the goal is to help your family restructure how it operates and create more healthy relationships.

Another common form of family therapy is *extended family systems therapy*, developed by psychiatrist Murray Bowen. This model examines how *differentiated* each member of the family is from one another, which means how distinct they are in terms of their thoughts, emotions, and decision-making ability. A family that is *fused* emotionally and cognitively, and who rarely disagree with one another or depart from the norms of the family, is said to form an *undifferentiated family ego mass*. One of the goals of working with a family like this is to help

129

each member find his or her own uniqueness and ability to think and behave outside the family. A therapist using this model often acts like a "coach" for the family, and he or she might initially work with one family member or with a couple.

Strategic family therapy, developed by psychologist Jay Haley, focuses on the way your family communicates. According to this treatment, the symptoms of the family's problem are actually failed attempts to change something in the family. A therapist using this method of treatment is very active with the family and will often assign tasks outside of therapy to help the family find a healthier way to communicate or to restructure itself. But don't be surprised if some of these requests sound a little strange at first. For example, a child who lights fires might be instructed to light more fires—under the guidance of his or her parents. The goal of such an intervention is to make the child grow bored with the activity and eventually stop doing it. Or, in another example, a couple who fights all the time might be instructed to go out to a very expensive dinner together each time they argue. Here the goal might be to make the fighting too expensive to continue.

> *In strategic family therapy, a couple who fights all the time might be instructed to go out to a very expensive dinner together each time they argue. Here the goal might be to make the fighting too expensive to continue.*

Narrative family therapy, largely developed by psychotherapist Michael White, examines the way family members tell the stories of their lives.

Your narrative family therapist will help you discover the various stories that make up your family as a whole. This can help redefine your family in some ways and give each member the opportunity to create new, alternative outcomes for their lives. In narrative therapy, your family members will also be instructed to think of the presenting problem as something outside of your family, instead of as a problem affecting just one individual member.

For example, if the presenting problem is a child with a behavioral problem, your narrative therapist will encourage your family to think of the behavioral problem as an external issue that is burdening both the child and the family. In this way, your family can unite with the child in addressing the issue, instead of blaming the child for the problem.

Many forms of family therapy use different methods of role-playing to examine communication styles and problem-solving skills, as well as to model new ways for family members to interact. Some family therapists might also ask you to create a family *genogram*, which is a generational map of relationships and difficulties. This can often be helpful because patterns sometimes become clearer, and the genogram can display problems that have been repeated throughout multiple generations of a family.

Family therapy is effective for treating:

- Family relationship problems
- Mental health problems involving children or dependent adults
- Mental health problems that are disrupting a family, such as depression, schizophrenia, or substance abuse

For more information, visit the websites of:

- The American Association for Marriage and Family Therapy: www.aamft.org

- The American Family Therapy Academy: www.afta.org

> **Now you try it:** *Ask each member of your family to write a story about how each member is getting along, and also write about any problems that might be present. Then, take some uninterrupted time to review the stories as a group, without judging each other, and try to incorporate each person's point of view into a new, unified, family narrative.*

CHAPTER 7

Good Health

B asic principles of a healthy lifestyle can go a long way toward supporting your mental health. Whether or not you're in therapy, taking medication, or both, paying attention to the basics of good health can make your treatment even more effective. In this chapter, you'll find some brief information on the importance of exercise, nutrition, stress reduction, and regular medical care.

EXERCISE

We've all heard the recommendations to get at least thirty minutes of daily aerobic exercise for a healthy heart. But who knew that mental health might be a bonus? Research has shown that exercise can reduce stress as well as symptoms of depression and anxiety, especially if you continue doing it for the long term. The most important factor is finding an exercise program that you're willing to commit to and that you enjoy.

For more information, visit the website of:

* The President's Council on Physical Fitness and Sports: www.fitness.gov. (Be sure to look at the link to "council publications.")

Now you try it: *Make a list of different types of exercise, such as walking, hiking, running, swimming, biking, dancing, working out at the gym, and so on. Rate each type of exercise according to how much you enjoy—or think you'd enjoy—the activity. Make a commitment to do this activity regularly, for at least thirty minutes, over the next two weeks. (Maybe you can begin by exercising three times the first week and four or five times the second. Make a commitment you can stick to.) At the same time, keep a diary of your mood each day. Do you notice any improvements after two weeks? If so, make it a regular part of your life.*

NUTRITION

Good nutrition is another important part of a healthy lifestyle and a healthy brain. A balanced diet should be low in fat, low in junk food, high in fiber, and include at least five servings of fruits and vegetables a day. Eating unhealthy foods and skipping meals can contribute to fluctuations in your mood and to low energy levels. For example, did you know that consuming too much caffeine can make you feel anxious or make your preexisting anxiety problem even worse? Plus, caffeine isn't only in coffee; it's also in tea, iced tea, sodas, energy drinks, and chocolate.

For more information, visit the website of:

- U. S. Department of Agriculture nutritional information: www.mypyramid.gov

Now you try it: *Make a list of everything you ate yesterday from the time you woke up until the time you went to bed. Look at your food intake critically. How many fruits and vegetables did you eat yesterday? How much sugar and caffeine did you consume? Did you eat at regular intervals, and was the food healthy? What healthy changes can you make?*

STRESS REDUCTION

In our busy daily lives, stress seems to be ever present. And stress can be a major contributor to many kinds of mental health problems. Human bodies are well adapted to dealing with stress in the short term. For example, if a tiger was running straight at you, wouldn't you want to have a fast heart and breathing rate, with blood pumping to all your muscles so that you could get away quickly from the danger? But what about after the tiger has gone? Wouldn't you hope that your body would return to its normal resting state? Unfortunately, for many of us, stress seems to be inescapable, and our bodies seldom return to the normal state of rest.

But, instead of letting stress control you, maybe you can find some simple ways to reduce the stress in your own life. Among the techniques we often recommend are getting regular exercise and engaging in pleasurable activities. We also recommend "taking ten"—ten quiet minutes a day for meditation, breathing, mindfulness practices, or daily prayer. Whichever you choose, the important thing is to make stress reduction a regular part of your daily routine and your life.

For more information, visit the website of:

- U. S. Navy Systematic Stress Management Program:
  www-nehc.med.navy.mil/hp/stress/StressMgmt.htm

Now you try it: *Take a few slow, long breaths. Imagine filling up your belly with air like a balloon. Breathe in through your nose for a count of three (count to yourself: "one, two, three"). Then, breathe out through your mouth or nose for a count of four (count to yourself: "one, two, three, four"). When your mind becomes distracted, refocus your attention on counting. You can say a calming word to yourself to help you relax, like "Peace," "Relax," or "Love." Continue this for about ten minutes. Notice any sensations of calmness or whether you feel more relaxed.*

REGULAR CHECKUPS

Many symptoms of mental health problems can be caused by physical problems in your body. For example, problems with your thyroid can cause symptoms of both depression and anxiety. Plus, there are many medications whose side effects can also mimic common mental health problems. If you have symptoms of a mental health problem, it's a good idea to get regular checkups from a medical professional, such as your primary care provider. You can discuss your symptoms and your current medications—including over-the-counter medicines, herbs, and supplements—and your medical professional may do some simple blood tests to rule out different causes of your problem.

For more information, visit the website of:

- WebMD checkup video:
  www.webmd.com/video/check-up-check-list

Now you try it: *Schedule a checkup with your physician or nurse practitioner today!*

CHAPTER 8

A Final Word About Medications

According to a 2004 poll sponsored in part by *Psychology Today* magazine, almost fifty-nine million adults in the United States sought treatment for a mental health problem between 2002 and 2004, and more than 80 percent of them took some kind of medication as a part of their treatment. However, for most people, medication is a confusing subject. To take or not to take, that is the question. So what should you do?

For the treatment of mental health problems, *psychotropic* medications can be used alone or in combination with therapy. In fact, for some problems, using a combination of medication and therapy may be the best treatment. This is especially true if you're struggling with specific problems like bipolar disorder and schizophrenia. In these cases, medication is the most important form of treatment. But using a

> *For most people, medication is a confusing subject. To take or not to take, that is the question.*

combination of medication and therapy is also important if you're struggling with a problem such as moderate to severe depression, especially if you're having suicidal thoughts. In this case, you might need the help of a medication to get you out of bed, get you activated in your life, and, perhaps, get you into a therapist's office. However, for other problems that are caused by distressing situations in your life—such as a difficult relationship—medication might be less important than therapy.

If you're having trouble making a decision about whether or not to take medication, we suggest that you discuss the issue with any medical or mental health professionals with whom you're already working, such as your primary care provider (PCP) or your therapist. You can also do your own research by reading medication reports and treatment recommendations issued by reputable sources (get started with the Web links at the end of this chapter).

However, even with all of this information available to you, the decision to use medication might still be confusing. You're bound to get different recommendations from different people. In order to help you make a more educated decision about medication, here are three important things we think you should keep in mind:

1.   First, you will need to keep taking your medication for it to be effective. *Psychotropic medications* such as antidepressants are not cures for mental health problems in the way that antibiotics kill germs and get rid of an infection. These medications work by increasing or decreasing certain chemicals in your brain called *neurotransmitters,* which affect your

mood. Psychotropic medications can improve your mood, make you feel better, and soothe your symptoms, but they will work only as long as you continue to take them. You may have to continue taking psychotropic medications for months or years, and, if you stop, your symptoms are likely to return.

Remember, you should never stop taking medications without first consulting a medical professional. Stopping your medications without medical advice can be extremely dangerous.

2. Second, most medications have side effects. Many people are often worried about the potential side effects of psychotropic medications. For some medications, such as antipsychotics, the side effects can be serious and long term. For others, such as some antianxiety and antidepressant medications, the side effects are less severe and often disappear over time. We understand why people are worried about these side effects; however, for some problems, medications are a necessity, and these side effects are often less troublesome than the problems the medications are meant to treat. Always discuss side effects with whoever prescribed your medication, because often there are simple solutions to these issues.

3. Third, medications sometimes have to be adjusted. If the side effects of your medication are difficult to tolerate, or the medication doesn't seem to be working, talk to your medical provider about adjusting the dosage or trying a different medication. Getting your

dosage right is often as much an art as it is a science, and there may be a similar medication you can try if you react poorly to the first one. Also, keep in mind that you might be prescribed more than one medication at a time, to give you the most effective treatment possible.

Ultimately, it's up to you to make the final decision about whether or not to use medication, but we strongly suggest that you listen to the advice of any medical and mental health professional(s) with whom you're working. We also urge you to consider the benefits of using medication, if it's recommended for you. Of course, you're bound to hear stories about people for whom medications didn't work, but there are also millions of people around the world for whom they do work—every day. And remember, for some problems, medication is the only treatment; for others, a combination of medications and therapy is recommended.

Remember, for some problems, medication is the only treatment; for others, a combination of medications and therapy is recommended.

Although it's clearly beyond the scope of this short chapter to provide you with all of the information on psychotropic medications, the following is a brief summary of some of the medications you might encounter.

Questions about psychotropic medication to ask your medical professional:

- What are some of the common side effects?

- Are there rare or serious side effects too?

- When should I expect it to begin working?

- Do I need any lab tests or special monitoring while I'm taking it?

- What should I do if I skip or miss a dose?

- What happens if I suddenly stop taking it?

- Does it interact with my other medications, herbs, or supplements?

- Is it possible to overdose on it?

- Is it covered by my insurance?

ANTIANXIETY MEDICATIONS

Three groups of medications are commonly used to treat anxiety: benzodiazepines, buspirone (BuSpar), and antidepressants. The first two groups are discussed below. The antidepressants are discussed in the next section.

Benzodiazepines are minor tranquilizers that induce sleep and relax muscles. Among the more common benzodiazepines are the following: alprazolam (Xanax), chlordiazepoxide (Librium), clonazepam (Klonopin), diazepam (Valium), lorazepam (Ativan), oxazepam (Serax), temazepam (Restoril), and triazolam (Halcion).

Buspirone (BuSpar) is an atypical antianxiety medication. This means that it decreases your anxiety level, without inducing sleep and muscle relaxation as the benzodiazepines do.

Some of the most common medications used in the treatment of anxiety problems are the *selective serotonin reuptake inhibitors* (SSRIs), which are discussed in the next section.

ANTIDEPRESSANT MEDICATIONS

There are four groups of medications used to treat depression: selective serotonin reuptake inhibitors, atypical antidepressants, tricyclic antidepressants, and monoamine oxidase inhibitors.

1. *Selective serotonin reuptake inhibitors* (SSRIs) are considered to be the first line of treatment for depression. As their name suggests, SSRIs increase the levels of the neurotransmitter serotonin. Among the more common SSRIs are citalopram (Celexa), escitalo-

pram (Lexapro), fluoxetine (Prozac), fluvoxamine (Luvox), paroxetine (Paxil), and sertraline (Zoloft).

2.   *Atypical antidepressants* are newer medications that work in unique ways. Venlafaxine (Effexor), duloxetine (Cymbalta), and mirtazapine (Remeron) increase the levels of the neurotransmitters serotonin and norepinephrine. Bupropion (Wellbutrin) is another atypical antidepressant that is thought to increase the levels of the neurotransmitters norepinephrine and dopamine.

3.   *Tricyclic antidepressants* (TCAs) are often used after multiple attempts to use SSRIs and atypical antidepressants have failed. TCAs were developed in the late 1950s, and the name refers to their chemical structure. Like the SSRIs, the TCAs are a family of related antidepressants. TCAs increase the levels of the neurotransmitter serotonin and/ or norepinephrine, but they aren't used as a first-line treatment for depression because they can also create a number of serious side effects.

    Some of the common TCAs include amitriptyline (Elavil), clomipramine (Anafranil), doxepin (Sinequan), imipramine (Tofranil), and nortriptyline (Pamelor).

4.   Finally, the last group of antidepressants is the oldest group, *monoamine oxidase inhibitors* (MAOIs). MAOIs were developed in the 1950s, and they too help increase the levels of serotonin, norepineph-

rine, and dopamine. Although they can be effective at treating some types of difficult depression, the potential side effects of MAOIs, coupled with necessary dietary restrictions, often outweigh the benefits of their use. Among the more commonly prescribed MAOIs are isocarboxazid (Marplan), phenelzine (Nardil), and tranylcypromine (Parnate).

ANTIMANIA MEDICATIONS

Antimania medications are often called mood stabilizers. The most common is lithium (Eskalith, Lithobid), a naturally occurring substance. It's not exactly clear how it reduces mood swings, but lithium generally begins to lessen symptoms of mania within one to three weeks, although it may take longer to fully control your mania. And it's reported to be effective in as many as 60 to 80 percent of the patients treated. Valproic acid (Depakene) and divalproex sodium (Depakote) are medications used to treat seizures that are also approved by the FDA to treat mania. Valproic acid is often used to treat patients when lithium has proven ineffective. Carbamazepine (Tegretol) is another antiseizure medication that has proven effective for the treatment of mania.

ANTIPSYCHOTIC MEDICATIONS

Antipsychotic medications are also known as *neuroleptics* or *major tranquilizers* because they have a very calming effect on people who take them. The medications often cause sleepiness, emotional soothing, and a lessening of agitation. These medications, used to treat schizophrenia and other psychoses, can be divided into two groups: traditional and atypical medications. Both groups of medication reduce the level of the neurotransmitter dopamine, and some atypicals also reduce the level of serotonin.

Both traditional and atypical medications lessen the severity of hallucinations, diminish delusions, and calm disturbed thinking. The newer atypical medications may also improve symptoms such as low energy, lack of emotion, lack of expressiveness, and lack of interest.

Among the more commonly prescribed traditional antipsychotic medications are chlorpromazine (Thorazine), fluphenazine (Prolixin), haloperidol (Haldol), thioridazine (Mellaril), and trifluoperazine (Stelazine).

Among the more commonly prescribed atypical antipsychotic medications are aripiprazole (Abilify), clozapine (Clozaril), olanzapine (Zyprexa), quetiapine (Seroquel), risperidone (Risperdal), and ziprasidone (Geodon).

Remember that the information in this chapter is very limited in scope. So be sure to ask the medical professional who prescribed your medication about how and when to take it and any common or expected side effects.

For more information, visit the websites of:

- National Alliance on Mental Illness: www.nami.org/ Content/NavigationMenu/Inform_Yourself/About_ Medications/Default798.htm

- National Institute of Mental Health: www.nimh.nih.gov/publicat/medicate.cfm

- Food and Drug Administration: www.fda.gov

CHAPTER 9

Famously Failed Therapies

In this chapter, you'll learn about some famously failed therapies. Unfortunately, most of them are still around, even though we wish they'd go the way of the dodo bird.

The failed treatments may seem to have little in common at first. But on second look, they generally share a "one size fits all" approach to therapy. These treatments have been purported to be useful for almost every mental health problem—and most physical health problems too. These failed treatments are also famous for claiming effectiveness based on the personal experience of their "inventor" or "discoverer," not because of scientific research. In general, the treatments in this chapter are agreed upon by the psychological community to be unproven and, in some cases, even dangerous.

So why is it important to read about famously failed treatments? As you can see from reading this book, there are an abundance of therapies to choose from as a consumer. So why waste your time and money with a therapy that is untested and unproven? With the exception of lobotomy, the treatments in this chapter came out of—or were popularized—during the 1970s, a time when many people were seeking ways to become more happy, creative, and fulfilled.

First, you'll be introduced to the psychosurgical technique of lobotomy popularized by the ice-pick-wielding Dr. Walter Freeman. Then, you'll become acquainted with Wilhelm Reich's orgone therapy in a box, Arthur Janov's screaming primal therapy, and, finally, the ever-evolving rebirthing therapy made famous by the supposedly immortal Leonard Orr.

Although you may not have been familiar with these famously failed therapies until now, there are many others you've probably heard of that we don't even have space to include. Does past-life regression therapy ring a bell? What about using hypnosis to recover memories of abuse or UFOs? How about angel therapy? These treatments might be fun if you're just looking for some laughs or to satisfy your curiosity, but they are not proven treatments for serious mental health problems like depression, anxiety, and so forth. Yet these therapies—and many more—continue to be a part of our self-help, quick-fix culture. So be careful when you choose an unproven treatment for your mental health problems, because the most popular therapy this year might be the primal scream of tomorrow.

Be careful when you choose an unproven treatment for your mental health problems, because the most popular therapy this year might be the primal scream of tomorrow.

LOBOTOMY

Lobotomy is a surgical procedure that makes cuts in parts of the brain believed to be associated with emotions and personality in order to cause changes in a person's behavior or feelings. Egas Moniz, a Portuguese neurologist, developed lobotomy (or *leucotomy* as he called it) in its most modern form. However, it was Walter Freeman, a psychiatrist and neurologist, who is credited with lobotomy's rise and spread across the United States. Freeman, along with neurosurgeon James Watts, performed the first prefrontal lobotomy in the United States in 1936.

Also termed *psychosurgery*, lobotomy involved boring holes into the skull of the patient to cut nerve fibers and tissue in the frontal lobes of the brain. Over time, Freeman "evolved" his technique into the *transorbital lobotomy* so that it could be accomplished more easily. Instead of drilling holes in the skull, he accessed the patient's brain through the eye socket with the use of an instrument like an ice pick. In fact, the first time Freeman performed this adapted lobotomy, his tool was an actual ice pick from his own kitchen!

Lobotomy was initially considered by Freeman and Watts to be a treatment of last resort. Keep in mind that modern-day treatments like the many different forms of psychotherapy and medication were not yet available. So a "treatment of last resort" was tried when "remedies" such as alternating blows to the head, immersion in freezing baths of water, medicines to induce convulsions, insulin-induced coma, and electroshock treatments didn't work. Lobotomy was frequently performed on patients with diagnoses like schizophrenia, obsessive-compulsive disorder, depression, and anxiety.

Over time, Freeman changed his belief about the utility of lobotomy and he began recommending it earlier in the course of a mental health problem as a "preventative" treatment. In the end, Freeman not only performed lobotomies on patients with severe mental health problems but also on people with epilepsy, chronic pain, behavioral problems, and mental retardation. Even children were counted among his patients! Lobotomy was performed on women at twice the rate that of men, and some patients received lobotomies two and even three times!

The potential side effects of cutting the frontal lobes of patients' brains turned out to be enormous. Many patients died. Others experienced hemorrhaging, seizures, incontinence, partial paralysis, disorientation, personality changes, inertia, memory loss, and a return of the symptoms of the mental health problems that the lobotomy had been intended to fix.

When Freeman performed lobotomies with Watts, they were done under anesthesia. Eventually, performing transorbital lobotomies on his own, Freeman used electroshock to anesthetize his patients. Most likely this had more to do with convenience for him than appropriate treatment for the patient, since he was fond of performing transorbital lobotomy in his outpatient office; a practice that created a rift between Freeman and Watts. Freeman was even known to experiment with local anesthesia during lobotomy—keeping the patient awake to determine the "optimal" amount of brain damage!

The audacity! According to author Jack El-Hai, in his book *The Lobotomist*, Freeman once ran into severe complications while performing a lobotomy on a female patient who began to bleed excessively. But rather than stopping the hemorrhage, Freeman first went to the waiting room, where he made sure that the patient's husband would be willing to spend the $1,000 necessary to stop the bleeding that Freeman had caused.

Lobotomy had its heyday in the 1940s and 1950s. Perhaps its most famous recipient (or victim) was Rose Kennedy, the twenty-three-year-old elder sister of President John F. Kennedy. Psychosurgery left Rose Kennedy with diminished mental capacity, barely able to speak and unable to care for herself.

Freeman has been described as a showman, performing multiple procedures a day as he spread his technique in lobotomy road shows across the country. At times, he even used two hands, cutting both the right and left frontal lobe simultaneously. He called the procedure a "time-saver." Lobotomy's mainstream acceptance was solidified when Egas Moniz, Freeman's predecessor, won the Nobel Prize for his "advances" in psychosurgery in 1949. Afterwards, the worldwide rates of lobotomy skyrocketed. (Recently, relatives of lobotomy sufferers have asked for Moniz's Nobel Prize to be revoked.) Ultimately, approximately fifty thousand lobotomies were performed in the United States between 1936 and the 1970s by thousands of surgeons.

But lobotomy was controversial even in the 1930s. Other professionals questioned the ethics of destroying healthy brain tissue and permanently changing the personalities of patients with mental health problems. Many also wondered whether patients who were severely ill could adequately give consent for this radical treatment and expressed concern that relatives with ulterior motives might authorize lobotomy despite the patient's best interest. Freeman himself was also examined and criticized since he had no formal training in surgery and no qualifications as a neurosurgeon! But the popularity of the practice won out and lobotomies continued for decades.

The decline of lobotomy began in 1954 when the medication Thorazine became available and largely replaced lobotomy as a treatment for symptoms of severe mental health problems. By the 1970s, courts and federal and state governments became involved in limiting the practice of lobotomy, and several countries banned its practice.

Although lobotomy is generally no longer practiced, psychosurgery itself is still around. Brain surgery for mental health problems has recently reappeared in some severe and otherwise untreatable cases of obsessive-compulsive disorder.

So why doesn't lobotomy work? Many of Freeman's contemporaries questioned lobotomy even during its rise and mainstream acceptance. Lobotomy was never subjected to rigorous scientific study, and its effectiveness has always been questionable. Although some patients and their families say that they benefited from the procedure, countless more were irreparably harmed—or even died—as a result of lobotomy. Of those patients who survived the procedure intact and without severe side effects, many saw the symptoms of their mental health problems return weeks or months after their lobotomy.

What's the bottom line? Lobotomy was an unscientific procedure used much too frequently and without good reason. Although many people with mental health problems have real chemical changes in their brain, destroying the brain's frontal lobes is no solution.

For more information, visit the websites of:

- Support group for family members of lobotomy sufferers: www.psychosurgery.org

- National Public Radio story: www.npr.org
  (search "lobotomy")

Now you try it: *On second thought ... please don't.*

ORGONE THERAPY

Orgone therapy was developed by Wilhelm Reich, a controversial Eastern European psychiatrist, psychoanalyst, and one-time follower of Sigmund Freud. In the 1930s, Reich claimed he'd discovered *orgone energy*, which he said was the vital, cosmic, universal force that permeates everything, including the human body. Reich believed that orgone energy could become blocked in the body and produce imbalances that result in psychological and physical health problems. Not only did Reich develop a psychotherapeutic treatment related to orgone energy, he also invented a series of "machines" that clients could use to harness orgone for self-healing.

One such technology was the *orgone accumulator*, also called the *orgone box*, which could be built by just about anyone. The orgone box was simply a wooden box lined with metal. Clients were instructed to sit inside the box for about one-half hour daily to absorb the healing properties of orgone. In the 1950s, the Food and Drug Administration (FDA) thought Reich had gone too far with the claims that the orgone accumulator could cure cancer and won a court injunction to ban the interstate sale of orgone boxes. Reich and his followers continually disputed that he had ever made such claims, and they continued to ship his machines. As a result, Reich was sentenced to two years in jail for contempt of court, where he died of heart failure in 1957 at the age of sixty. While he was in jail, the government conducted a mass book burning of all Reich's work related to orgone energy.

Aside from the orgone box, Reich also developed a framework for psychotherapy. Still practiced by some psychiatrists today, orgone therapy contends that mental health can be achieved when blocked orgone energy in the body is released. Different techniques are used to undo what he called *character armor* and *body armor*, characteristics that arise in the individual due to stuck energy. Reich believed that body armor was formed in childhood in response to the repression of basic instincts and desires in order to conform to adult society and cultural norms. Body armor might present itself as muscle spasms or tightness, inability to attain orgasm, or walking, talking, or breathing in a certain way.

Orgone therapy aims to eliminate both types of armor. The orgone therapist might use talk therapy to work at issues involving character, and "hands-on" methods to help the client chip away at body armor. Some of orgone therapy's talk therapy techniques are eerily similar to primal therapy, with stories of howling and screaming patients who kick and punch pillows and uncover painful memories.

Clients in orgone therapy may be assessed and treated by their orgone therapist only in their underclothes. The therapist might probe, pinch, or press on painful or sensitive places like the calves, neck, or stomach to get the client to express emotions like anger or rage. As in, "Ouch! That hurts! What the $%@# are you doing to me?" The expression of these emotions is said to help restore the proper flow of orgone energy and remove the underlying causes of the mental health problem. Other ways that orgone energy is rebalanced or unblocked include repeatedly opening the eyes wide, grimacing and frowning, and initiating the gag reflex by inducing vomiting ... all during the therapy session!

So why doesn't orgone therapy work? Do we really need to explain it? Although Reich's orgone energy might remind you of some other ancient energy systems, such as Indian *prana* or Chinese *chi*, we recommend seeking out therapies that have been tested and proven effective. As with most of our "failed therapies," orgone therapy is not the be-all and end-all solution for all mental health problems. At best, it is an experimental and not scientifically validated treatment that requires informed consent from the consumer. Although many people with mental health problems might have muscle tension or related somatic symptoms such as physical pain, there are much better treatments described in this book that shouldn't be ignored in favor of an experimental approach.

However, Reich's work did give rise to countless types of body-oriented therapy. His concept of *body armor* persists, and many different types of effective therapy, including cognitive behavioral therapy, also aim to help clients free up muscular tension and improve breathing patterns in order to help them feel better. He certainly had the right idea there. But just because emotions are released when certain patterns of breathing are changed, or feelings come up when muscle spasms let go, these mini-cathartic experiences are not treatments in and of themselves.

As for enduring physically painful therapy sessions at the hands of your orgone therapist, the old adage rings true: if it looks like a duck, walks like a duck, and quacks like a duck, it's probably a duck. So is the case with orgone therapy: if it feels painful and humiliating, chances are this therapy isn't going to be good for you.

So, does the orgone accumulator harness vital energy? Maybe, maybe not. Should you consider this as an effective treatment for a mental health problem? Definitely not.

What's the bottom line? Spending some time in an orgone box might help you sweat off a few pounds and force you to sit still for a while, but if you're seeking treatment for a mental health problem that's

---

E=mc what? Reich once tried to get Albert Einstein to validate the existence of orgone energy by proving that there was a temperature difference above the orgone accumulator. But when one of Einstein's assistants realized that the phenomenon was caused by heat reflecting off the ceiling, Einstein stopped communicating with Reich.

affecting your life, seek professional help somewhere else ... outside the box!

For more information, visit the websites of:

- The American College of Orgonomy: www.orgonomy.org
- The Institute for Orgonomic Science: www.orgonomicscience.org

> **Now you try it:** *Get some wood. Make a box. Line it with metal (the more layers, the more power!). Sit in it for thirty minutes a day. Did it solve your problems? We didn't think so.*

PRIMAL THERAPY

Primal therapy was popularized by psychologist Arthur Janov after a client let out a bloodcurdling scream in session that, supposedly, shook the walls of Janov's room. After this deafening moment, the client said that he could finally feel his emotions, while Janov, perhaps feeling lucky, went on to publish *The Primal Scream* in 1970, inspiring great popular interest and even greater professional skepticism.

Since then, Janov has devoted his life to practicing and teaching primal therapy at the Primal Center in Los Angeles, which claims to help people resolve deep and painful emotions. Janov claims in his books not only that primal therapy cures *all* mental illness, but that it is the *one and only* therapy that can do so.

The theory behind primal therapy is that all mental health problems come from early experiences of children not getting their needs met by their parents. This is called *primal pain*. According to primal therapy, you can improve your mental health only after you express your "real needs and pains." Janov believes that feeling the pain of a difficult experience or memory as an adult takes the pain out of the memory

Supposedly, primal therapy involves a client tapping into deeply painful feelings and expressing them during the session. This might involve crying, sobbing, screaming, calling out to "Mommy" or "Daddy," writhing, kicking, convulsing, and other expressions of intense emotion. Primal therapy is usually conducted in a soundproof room to allow for the screaming and crying that are its common features. At the Primal Center, a person might also expect to have his or her blood pressure, temperature, and heart rate taken before and after the session to make sure the treatment is "working."

The client's experience is generally described as *catharsis* (although Janov claims that *true* primal therapy is much more than just catharsis).

After this primal experience, clients are said to relive painful life experiences through vivid memories, after which the client feels calmer, clearer, and happier.

Primal therapy treatment involves an incredible commitment of time, energy, and money. In the first three weeks, intensive individual therapy is scheduled for about two hours per day. After that, individual and group therapy—each at least once a week—continue for a year. However, some clients have reportedly been in primal therapy for more than ten years. Primal therapy is so time-consuming that the Primal Center's website recommends that clients move to Los Angeles and plan to stay for about one year. The Primal Center's website also says that clients should be able to return to work after a few weeks. And return to work you must, since the first three weeks of intensive therapy will run you about $6,000. Stories abound about clients taking extra low-paying jobs and selling their houses just to afford the high cost and frequency of primal therapy.

So why doesn't primal therapy work? The psychological community generally agrees that catharsis—in and of itself—is not a valid therapy. In fact, social psychologists such as Brad Bushman have shown that expressions of anger can lead to more anger, not less. Basically, just because a person feels an emotion, or reexperiences a painful event, that doesn't mean he or she will recover or that the symptoms of the mental health problem will disappear. In fact, repeatedly experiencing

---

The fans weren't the only ones screaming. One of primal therapy's most famous clients was former Beatles member John Lennon, who underwent an abbreviated course of primal therapy with Janov in the 1970s. In interviews, Lennon repeatedly said that primal therapy helped him release painful feelings from his childhood.

intense and painful emotions and memories may make you feel worse. What's more, primal therapy as a whole is not scientifically validated, meaning there aren't good quality scientific studies that demonstrate it works well as a treatment for any mental health problems.

What's the bottom line? Even though some people may have found primal therapy helpful, it's an untested treatment that might leave you screaming for something better.

For more information, visit the websites of:

- Dr. Arthur Janov's Primal Center: www.primaltherapy.com
- The Primal Institute: www.primalinstitute.com

Now you try it: *Think of something that makes you angry. Scream. Scream some more. Besides making your voice hoarse, did it help you cope with the situation in a healthier way? We didn't think so.*

REBIRTHING

Developed in the 1970s by Leonard Orr, a born-again Christian turned New Age self-help guru, *rebirthing* is a dubious process of healing that uses an allegedly special type of breathing. Orr invented rebirthing after soaking in his bathtub for many hours, during which time he supposedly remembered and reexperienced the trauma of his own birth, somewhere around the time he was thirty-five years old.

Apparently, this highly improbable memory brought Orr some relief in his life, and, thus, another "treatment" was born. Orr theorized that the *birth trauma* he had reexperienced in his tub was the origin of all his emotional and physical difficulties, and he soon began rebirthing others. His first clients also claimed to reexperience memories of their own births, which released them from their own problems, and, soon, the baby boomers were giving birth to themselves once again.

Generally speaking, Orr's theory is that birth trauma affects breathing patterns, which block energy in the body, and manifests as mental and physical problems. (Does this sound familiar? Remember orgone therapy?) Rebirthing purports to teach clients a new way of breathing that includes breathing not just air, but energy too. According to Orr, not only can rebirthing heal trauma and other psychological and physical difficulties, it can also reverse aging!

Rebirthing began as a technique that was done while the client was immersed in water (using a snorkel and nose plugs) and eventually graduated to a breathing technique done on a bed ("dry rebirthing") individually or in a group setting. A client can expect about ten one-hour sessions at first, graduating to another ten sessions, and then continuing to practice at home.

Orr and his most famous student, Sondra Ray, still continue to train professional "rebirthers" around the world. Orr's theory and practice might now be best described as "everything but the kitchen sink." *Rebirthing-breathing*, a technique that focuses on upper-chest

Full of hot air? Both Leonard Orr and Sondra Ray claim that immortality is possible and say that the act of dying is a choice we all make. On his website, Orr poses this question: "Which statement do you choose to believe? Death is inevitable and beyond my control or Death is optional and self-created." If they live forever, and rebirthing works, Orr and Ray will have the last laugh. Only time will tell.

breathing, is only one part of his current program. Followers are also advised to follow a vegetarian diet, get plenty of exercise, bathe twice a day, sit regularly by an open fire, seek out a spiritual guide, and so forth. Most of these elements sounds pretty good to us … but they sound more like components of a healthy lifestyle than rebirthing.

Unfortunately, though, there are many therapists hanging out shingles as professional rebirthers, only some of whom focus on the techniques that Orr and Ray popularized. Many rebirthers combine rebirthing therapy with *regression* and *reparenting* therapies that may end up leaving clients embarrassed, ashamed, and humiliated. In some cases, it also might leave them in diapers sucking on a baby bottle. These forms of therapy can be especially dangerous, causing a person to become increasingly dependent on the therapist. So beware!

The most notorious rebirthing case of all involved the 2001 death of ten-year-old Candace Newmaker, who was asphyxiated during an especially bizarre rebirthing session that was supposedly intended to increase her attachment to her adoptive mother. How it was supposed to do this, we don't know. Candace was wrapped in sheets and covered in pillows and asked to struggle her way out to be reborn, all the while being held down by several adults. Despite her pleas that she couldn't breathe, the adults continued smothering her. After being found guilty of "reckless child abuse resulting in death," the rebirthing therapists received sixteen-year prison sentences for their crimes. In response to this case, the state of Colorado banned harmful rebirthing practices and the American Psychiatric Association issued a press release warning the public about the dangers of rebirthing and other therapies involving restraining children.

So, why doesn't rebirthing work? Like the other failed therapies in this book, rebirthing has not been scientifically validated despite its thirty-year history. Aspects of Orr's philosophy clearly have a place in healthy living, and some of his core principles include theories about negative thought patterns. But this is nothing new. Many forms of cognitive behavior therapy will help you sort through negative thought patterns and belief systems, albeit with a different idea about their origin. And healthy living is important no matter what. So why not stick to the therapies that are backed by some solid research? This is important especially because there is no proof that changing your breathing pattern can actually free you from negative thoughts and mental health problems.

So, what's the bottom line? Rebirthing has some interesting holistic principles, but there's no evidence that changing breathing patterns alone will cure anyone of a mental (or physical) health problem. Moreover, there are versions of rebirthing that are downright dangerous and should be avoided at all costs.

For more information, visit the website of:

- Rebirthing-Breathwork with Leonard Orr: www.rebirthingbreathwork.com

- Sondra Ray: www.sondraray.com

> **Now you try it:** *Sit in a comfortable chair and breathe rather quickly through your mouth into your upper chest twenty times. Feel the energy flowing? Or, wait, maybe you're just feeling dizzy from all that hyperventilating?*

Further Reading and References

Bramlett, M. D., and W. D. Mosher. 2002. *Cohabitation, Marriage, Divorce, and Remarriage in the United States.* National Center for Health Statistics. Vital and Health Statistics 23(22).

Bushman, B. J. 2002. Does venting anger feed or extinguish the flame? Catharsis, rumination, distraction, anger, and aggressive responding. *Personality and Social Psychology Bulletin* 28(6):724-31.

Bushman, B. J., W. C. Pedersen, E. A. Vasquez, A. M. Bonacci, and N. Miller. 2005. Chewing on it can chew you up: Effects of rumination on displaced aggression triggered by a minor event. *Journal of Personality and Social Psychology* 88(6):969-83.

Couples in therapy. 2007. *Us,* August. Page 12.

El-Hai, J. 2005. *The Lobotomist: A Maverick Medical Genius and His Tragic Quest to Rid the World of Mental Illness*. Hoboken, New Jersey: John Wiley & Sons, Inc.

Elkin, I., M. T. Shea, J. T. Watkins, S. D. Imber, S. M. Sotsky, J. F. Collins, D. R. Glass, P. A. Pilkonis, W. R. Leber, and J. P. Docherty. 1989. National Institute of Mental Health treatment of depression collaborative research program: General effectiveness of treatments. *Archives of General Psychiatry* 46(11):971-82.

Frankl, V. E. 1984. *Man's Search for Meaning: An Introduction to Logotherapy*, 3rd ed. New York: Simon & Schuster.

Hall, D. E. 2006. Religious attendance: More cost-effective than Lipitor? *The Journal of the American Board of Family Medicine* 19:103.

Harris Interactive, *Psychology Today*, and PacifiCare Behavioral Health. 2004. *Therapy in America 2004*. http://cms.psychologytoday.com/pto/press_release_050404.html. Accesssed June 14, 2004.

Hornberger, R. H. 1959. The differential reduction of aggressive responses as a function of interpolated activities. *American Psychologist* 14:354.

Linehan, M. M. 1993. *Cognitive-Behavioral Treatment of Borderline Personality Disorder*. New York: The Guilford Press.

Maltby, J., C. A. Lewis, and L. Day. 1999. Religious orientation and psychological well-being: The role of the frequency of personal prayer. *British Journal of Health Psychology* 4: 363–78.

Mental health: Does therapy help? 1995. *Consumer Reports*, November, 734-39.

National Institute of Mental Health. 2001. The numbers count: Mental disorders in America. http://www.nimh.nih.gov/publicat/numbers.cfm. Accessed August 19, 2007.

Orlinsky, D., and K. Howard. 1986. Process and outcome in psycho-therapy. In *Handbook of Psychotherapy and Behavior Change.* Edited by S. L. Garfield and A. E. Bergin. New York: John Wiley and Sons.

Perls, L. 1978. An oral history of Gestalt therapy. Part I: A conversa-tion with Laura Perls, by Edward Rosenfeld. *The Gestalt Journal* 1:8-31.

Rusting, C. L., and S. Nolen-Hoeksema. 1998. Regulating responses to anger: Effects of rumination and distraction on angry mood. *Journal of Personality and Social Psychology* 74:790-803.

Seligman, M. E. P., T. A. Steen, N. Park, and C. Peterson. 2005. Positive psychology progress: Empirical validation of interventions. *American Psychologist* 60:410-21.

Simon, G., J. Savarino, B. Operskalski, and P. S. Wang. 2006. Suicide risk during antidepressant treatment. *American Journal of Psychiatry* 163:41-47.

Smith, M. L., and G. V. Glass. 1977. Meta-analysis of psychotherapy outcome studies. *American Psychologist* 32(9):752-60.

Wallis, C. 2005. The new science of happiness. *Time,* January, 25-8.

Wang, P. S., P. Berglund, M. Olfson, H. A. Pincus, K. B. Wells, and R. C. Kessler. 2005. Failure and delay in initial treatment contact after first onset of mental disorders in the National Comorbidity Survey replication. *Archives of General Psychiatry* 62:603-13.

Warga, C. 1988. You are what you think: An interview with Albert Ellis. *Psychology Today,* September, 54-58.

Jeffrey C. Wood, Psy.D., lives and works in the San Francisco Bay Area. He specializes in cognitive behavioral treatments for depression, anxiety, trauma, and chronic pain, as well as assertiveness and life-skills coaching. Wood is a part-time professor at the Wright Institute, a clinical psychology graduate school, in Berkeley, CA. He is author of *Getting Help* and coauthor of *The Dialectical Behavior Therapy Skills Workbook*.

Minnie Wood, NP, is an adult nurse practitioner. She is a primary care provider at a community health center in San Francisco where she also provides case management services to patients with chronic pain, substance abuse, and mental health issues.